Halsey, Roaalie V.
Forgotten Book s
of the American Nursery.

Forgotten Books of the American Nursery

The Devil and the Disobedient Child

FORGOTTEN BOOKS
OF
THE AMERICAN NURSERY

A History of the Development of the American Story-Book

BY

ROSALIE V. HALSEY

BOSTON

Charles E. Goodspeed & Co.

1911

Detroit: Reissued by Singing Tree Press, Book Tower, 1969

∴

Of this book seven hundred copies were printed in November 1911, by D. B. Updike, at The Merrymount Press, Boston

Library of Congress Catalog Card Number 68-31084

TABLE OF CONTENTS

ILLUSTRATIONS

Illustrations

Illustrations

CHAPTER I

Introductory

Thy life to mend
This *book* attend.

The New England Tutor
London (1702–14)

To be brought up in fear
And learn A B C.

FOXE, *Book of Martyrs*

Forgotten Books of the American Nursery

∴

CHAPTER I

Introductory

A SHELF full of books belonging to the American children of colonial times and of the early days of the Republic presents a strangely unfamiliar and curious appearance. If chronologically placed, the earliest coverless chap-books are hardly noticeable next to their immediate successors with wooden sides; and these, in turn, are dominated by the gilt, silver, and many colored bindings of diminutive dimensions which hold the stories dear to the childish heart from Revolutionary days to the beginning of the nineteenth century. Then bright blue, salmon, yellow, and marbled paper covers make a vivid display which, as the century grows older, fades into the sad-colored cloth bindings thought adapted to many children's books of its second quarter.

An examination of their contents shows them to be equally foreign to present day ideas as to the desirable characteristics for children's literature. Yet the crooked black type and crude illustrations of the wholly religious episodes related in the oldest volumes on the shelf, the didactic and moral stories with their tiny type-metal, wood, and copper-plate pictures of the next groups; and the "improving" American tales adorned with blurred colored engravings, or stiff steel and wood illustrations, that were produced for juvenile amusement in the early part of the nineteenth century,—all are as interesting to the lover of children as they are unattractive to the modern children themselves. The little ones very naturally find the stilted language of these old stories unintelligible and the artificial plots bewildering; but to one interested in the adult literature of the same periods of history an acquaintance with these amusement books of past generations has a peculiar charm and value of its own. They then become not merely curiosities, but the means of tracing the evolution of an American literature for children.

To the student desiring an intimate acquaintance with any civilized people, its lighter literature is always a great aid to personal research; the more trivial, the more detailed, the greater the worth to the investigator are these pen-pictures as records of the nation he wishes to know. Something of this value have the story-books of old-fashioned childhood. Trivial as they undoubtedly are, they nevertheless often contain our best sketches of child-life in the eighteenth and early nineteenth centuries,—a life as different from that of a twentieth century child as was the adult society of those old days from that of the present time. They also enable us to mark as is possible in no other way, the gradual development of a body of writing which, though lagging much behind the adult literature, was yet also affected by the local and social conditions in America.

Without attempting to give the history of the evolution of the A B C book in England—the legitimate ancestor of all juvenile books—two main topics must be briefly discussed before entering upon the proper matter of this volume. The first relates to the family life in the early days of the

Massachusetts Commonwealth, the province that produced the first juvenile book. The second topic has to do with the literature thought suitable for children in those early Puritan days. These two subjects are closely related, the second being dependent upon the first. Both are necessary to the history of these quaint toy volumes, whose stories lack much meaning unless the conditions of life and literature preceding them are understood.

When the Pilgrim Fathers, seeking freedom of faith, founded their first settlements in the new country, one of their earliest efforts was directed toward firmly establishing their own religion. This, though nominally free, was eventually, under the Mathers, to become a theocracy as intolerant as that faith from which they had fled. The rocks upon which this religion was builded were the Bible and the Catechism. In this history of toy-books the catechism is, however, perhaps almost the more important to consider, for it was a product of the times, and regarded as indispensable to the proper training of a family.

The Puritan conception of life, as an error to be rectified by suffering rather than as a joy to be accepted with thanksgiving, made the preparation for death and the dreadful Day of Judgment the chief end of existence. The catechism, therefore, with its fear-inspiring description of Hell and the consequences of sin, became inevitably the chief means of instructing children in the knowledge of their sinful inheritance. In order to insure a supply of catechisms, it was voted by the members of the company in sixteen hundred and twenty-nine, when preparing to emigrate, to expend "3 shillings for 2 dussen and ten catechismes."* A contract was also made in the same year with "sundry intended ministers for catechising, as also in teaching, or causing to be taught the Companyes servants & their children, as also the salvages and their children."† Parents, especially the mothers, were continually exhorted in sermons preached for a century after the founding of the colony, to catechize the children every day, "that," said Cotton Mather, "you may be continually dropping something of the *Catechism* upon them: Some Honey out of the Rock"! Indeed, the learned divine seems to have regarded it as a soothing and toothsome morsel, for he even imagined that the children cried for it continuously, saying: "*O our dear Parents, Acquaint us with the Great God. . . . Let us not go from your Tender Knees, down to the Place of Dragons. Oh! not Parents, but Ostriches: Not Parents, but Prodigies.*"‡

Much dissension soon arose among the ministers of the settlements as to which catechism should be taught. As the result of the discussion the "General Corte," which met in sixteen hundred and forty-one, "desired that the elders would make a catechism for *the instruction of youth in the grounds of religion.*" §

To meet this request, several clergymen immediately responded. Among them was John Cotton, who presumably prepared a small volume which was entitled "*Milk for Babes.* Drawn out of the Breast of Both Testaments. Chiefly for the spiritual nourishment of *Boston* Babes in either England: But may be of like use for any children." For the present purpose

* *Records of Mass. Bay*, vol. i, p. 37 h.

† *Ibid.*, vol. i, p. 37 e.

‡ Ford, *The New England Primer*, p. 83.

§ *Records of Mass. Bay*, vol. i, p. 328.

the importance of this little book lies in the supposition that it was printed at Cambridge, by Daye, between sixteen hundred and forty-one and sixteen hundred and forty-five, and therefore was the first book of any kind written and printed in America for children;—an importance altogether different from that attached to it by the author's grandson, Cotton Mather, when he asserted that "Milk for Babes" would be "valued and studied and improved till New England cease to be New England."*

To the little colonials this "Catechism of New England" was a great improvement upon any predecessor, even upon the Westminster Shorter Catechism, for it reduced the one hundred and seven questions of that famous body of doctrine to sixty-seven, and the longest answer in "Milk for Babes" contained only eighty-four words.†

As the century grew older other catechisms were printed. The number produced before the eighteenth century bears witness to the diverse views in a community in which they were considered an essential for every member, adult or child. Among the six hundred titles roughly computed as the output of the press by seventeen hundred in the new country, eleven different catechisms may be counted, with twenty editions in all; of these the titles of four indicate that they were designed for very little children. In each community the pastor appointed the catechism to be taught in the school, and joined the teacher in drilling the children in its questions and answers. Indeed, the answers were regarded as irrefutable in those uncritical days, and hence a strong shield and buckler

* Ford, *The New England Primer*, p. 92. † *Ibid.*

against manifold temptations provided by "yt ould deluder Satan." To offset the task of learning these doctrines of the church, it is probable that the mothers regaled the little ones with old folk-lore tales when the family gathered together around the great living-room fire in the winter evening, or asked eagerly for a bedtime story in the long summer twilight. Tales such as "Jack the Giant Killer," "Tom Thumb," the "Children in the Wood," and "Guy of Warwick," were orally current even among the plain people of England, though frowned upon by many of the Puritan element. Therefore it is at least presumable that these were all familiar to the colonists. In fact, it is known that John Dunton, in sixteen hundred and eighty-six, sold in his Boston warehouse "The History of Tom Thumb," which he facetiously offered to an ignorant customer "in folio with Marginal notes." Besides these orally related tales of enchantment, the children had a few simple pastimes, but at first the few toys were necessarily of home manufacture. On the whole, amusements were not encouraged, although "In the year sixteen hundred and ninety-five Mr. Higginson," writes Mrs. Earle, "wrote from Massachusetts to his brother in England, that if toys were imported in small quantity to America, they would sell." And a venture of this character was certainly made by seventeen hundred and twelve in Boston. Still, these were the exception in a commonwealth where amusements were considered as wiles of the Devil, against whom the ministers constantly warned the congregations committed to their charge.

Home in the seventeenth century—and indeed in the eighteenth century—was a place where for children the rule "to be seen, not heard," was strictly enforced. To read Judge Sewall's diary is to be convinced that for children to obtain any importance in life, death was necessary. Funerals of little ones were of frequent occurrence, and were conducted with great ceremony, in which pomp and meagre preparation were strangely mingled. Baby Henry Sewall's funeral procession, for instance, included eight ministers, the governor and magistrates of the county, and two nurses who bore the little body to the grave, into which, half full of water from the raging storm, the rude coffin was lowered. Death was kept before the eyes of every member of the colony; even two-year-old babies learned such mournful verse as this:

"I, in the Burying Place may See
Graves Shorter than I;
From Death's Arreſt no age is free
Young Children too may die;
My God, may such an awful Sight
Awakening be to me!
Oh! that by Grace I might
For Death prepared be."

When the younger members of the family are otherwise mentioned in the Judge's diary, it is perhaps to note the parents' pride in the eighteen-months-old infant's knowledge of the catechism, an acquirement rewarded by the gift of a red apple, but which suggests the reason for many funerals. Or, again, difficulties with the alphabet are sorrowfully put down; and also delinquencies at the age of four in attending family prayer, with a full account of punishments meted out to the culprit. Such details are, indeed, but natural, for under the stern conditions imposed by Cotton and the Mathers, religion looms large in the foreground of any sketch of family life handed down from the first century of the Massachusetts colony. Perhaps the very earliest picture in which a colonial child with a book occupies the centre of the canvas is that given in a letter of Samuel Sewall's. In sixteen hundred and seventy-one he wrote with pride to a friend of "little Betty, who though Reading passing well, took Three Moneths to Read the first Volume of the Book of Martyrs" as she sat by the fire-light at night after her daily task of spinning was done. Foxe's "Martyrs," seems gruesome reading for a little girl at bedtime, but it was so popular in England that, with the Bible and Catechism, it was included in the library of all households that could afford it.

Just ten years later, in sixteen hundred and eighty-one, Bunyan's "Pilgrim's Progress" was printed in Boston by Samuel Green, and, being easily obtainable, superseded in a measure the "Book of Martyrs" as a household treasure. Bunyan's dream, according to Macaulay, was the daily conversation of thousands, and was received in New England with far greater eagerness than in the author's own country. The children undoubtedly listened to the talk of their elders and gazed with wide-open eyes at the execrable plates in the imported editions illustrating Christian's journey. After the deaths by fire and sword of the Martyrs, the Pilgrim's difficulties in the Slough of Despond, or with the Giant Despair, afforded pleasurable reading; while Mr. Great Heart's courageous cheerfulness brought practically a new characteristic into Puritan literature.

To Bunyan the children in both old and New England

were indebted for another book, entitled "A Book for Boys and Girls: or, Country Rhimes for Children. By J. B. Licenſed and Entered according to Order."* Printed in London, it probably soon made its way to this country, where Bunyan was already so well known. "This little octavo volume," writes Mrs. Field in "The Child and his Book," "was considered a perfect child's book, but was in fact only the literary milk of the unfortunate babes of the period." In the light of modern views upon juvenile reading and entertainment, the Puritan ideal of mental pabulum for little ones is worth recording in an extract from the preface. The following lines set forth this author's three-fold purpose:

"To show them how each Fingle-fangle,
On which they doting are, their souls entangle,
As with a Web, a Trap, a Gin, or Snare.
While by their Play-things, I would them entice,
To mount their Thoughts from what are childiſh Toys
To Heaven for that 's prepar'd for Girls and Boys.
Nor do I so confine myself to theſe
As to shun graver things, I seek to pleaſe,
Thoſe more compoſ'd with better things than Toys:
Tho thus I would be catching Girls and Boys."

In the seventy-four Meditations composing this curious medley—"tho but in Homely Rhimes"—upon subjects familiar to any little girl or boy, none leaves the moral to the imagination. Nevertheless, it could well have been a relaxation, after the daily drill in "A B abs" and catechism, to turn the leaves and to spell out this:

* In the possession of the British Museum.

UPON THE FROG

The Frog by nature is both damp and cold,
Her mouth is large, her belly much will hold,
She sits somewhat aſcending, loves to be
Croaking in gardens tho' unpleaſantly.

Compariſon

The hypocrite is like unto this frog;
As like as is the Puppy to the Dog.
He is of nature cold, his mouth is wide
To prate, and at true Goodneſs to deride.

Doubtless, too, many little Puritans quite envied the child in "The Boy and the Watchmaker," a jingle wherein the former said, among other things:

"This Watch my Father did on me beſtow
A Golden one it is, but 't will not go,
Unleſs it be at an Uncertainty;
I think there is no watch as bad as mine.
Sometimes 't is sullen, 't will not go at all,
And yet 't was never broke, nor had a fall."

The same small boys may even have enjoyed the tedious explanation of the mechanism of the time-piece given by the *Watchmaker*, and after skipping the "Comparison" (which made the boy represent a convert and the watch in his pocket illustrative of "Grace within his Heart"), they probably turned eagerly to the next Meditation *Upon the Boy and his Paper of Plumbs*. Weather-cocks, Hobby-horses, Horses, and Drums, all served Bunyan in his effort "to point a moral" while adorning his tales.

In a later edition of these grotesque and quaint conceptions, some alterations were made and a primer was included. It then appeared as "A Book for Boys and Girls; or Temporal Things Spiritualized;" and by the time the ninth edition was reached, in seventeen hundred and twenty-four, the book was hardly recognizable as "Divine Emblems; or Temporal Things Spiritualized."

At present there is no evidence that these rhymes were printed in the colonies until long after this ninth edition was issued. It is possible that the success attending a book printed in Boston shortly after the original "Country Rhimes" was written, made the colonial printers feel that their profit would be greater by devoting spare type and paper to the now famous "New England Primer." Moreover, it seems peculiarly in keeping with the cast of the New England mind of the eighteenth century that although Bunyan had attempted to combine play-things with religious teaching for the English children, for the little colonials the first combination was the elementary teaching and religious exercises found in the great "Puritan Primer." Each child was practically, if not verbally, told that

"This little Catechism learned by heart (for so it ought)
The Primer next commanded is for Children to be taught."

The Primer, however, was not a product wholly of New England. In sixteen hundred and eighty-five there had been printed in Boston by Green, "The Protestant Tutor for Children," a primer, a mutilated copy of which is now owned by the American Antiquarian Society. "This," again to quote Mr. Ford, "was probably an abridged edition of a book bearing the same title, printed in London, with the expressed design of bringing up children in an aversion to Popery." In Protestant New England the author's purpose naturally called forth profound approbation, and in "Green's edition of the Tutor lay the germ of the great picture alphabet of our fore-fathers."* The author, Benjamin Harris, had immigrated to Boston for personal reasons, and coming in contact with the residents, saw the latent possibilities in "The Protestant Tutor." "To make it more salable," writes Mr. Ford in "The New England Primer," "the school-book character was increased, while to give it an even better chance of success by an appeal to local pride it was rechristened and came forth under the now famous title of 'The New England Primer.'"†

A careful examination of the titles contained in the first volume of Evans's "American Bibliography" shows how exactly this infant's primer represented the spirit of the times. This chronological list of American imprints of the first one hundred years of the colonial press is largely a record in type of the religious activity of the country, and is impressive as a witness to the obedience of the press to the law of supply and demand. With the Puritan appetite for a grim religion served in sermons upon every subject, ornamented and seasoned with supposedly apt Scriptural quotations, a demand was created for printed discourses to be read and inwardly digested at home. This demand the printers supplied. Amid such literary conditions the primer came as light food for infants' minds, and as such was accepted by parents to impress religious ideas when teaching the alphabet.

It is not by any means certain that the first edition of this great primer of our ancestors contained illustrations, as en-

* Ford, *The New England Primer*, p. 38. † *Ibid.*

gravers were few in America before the eighteenth century. Yet it seems altogether probable that they were introduced early in the next century, as by seventeen hundred and seventeen Benjamin Harris, Jr., had printed in Boston "The Holy Bible in Verse," containing cuts identical with those in "The New England Primer" of a somewhat later date, and these pictures could well have served as illustrations for both these books for children's use, profit, and pleasure. At all events, the thorough approval by parents and clergy of this small schoolbook soon brought to many a household the novelty of a real picture-book.

Hitherto little children had been perforce content with the few illustrations the adult books afforded. Now the printing of this tiny volume, with its curious black pictures accompanying the text of religious instruction, catechism, and alphabets, marked a milestone on the long lane that eventually led to the well-drawn pictures in the modern books for children.

It is difficult at so late a day to estimate correctly the pleasure this famous picture alphabet brought to the various colonial households. What the original illustrations were like can only be inferred from those in "The Holy Bible in Verse," and in later editions of the primer itself. In the Bible Adam (or is it Eve?) stands pointing to a tree around which a serpent is coiled. By seventeen hundred and thirty-seven the engraver was sufficiently skilled to represent two figures, who stand as colossal statues on either side of the tree whose fruit had had such disastrous effects. However, at a time when art criticism had no terrors for the engraver, it could well have been a delight to many a family of little ones to gaze upon

"The Lion bold
The Lamb doth hold"

and to speculate upon the exact place where the lion ended and the lamb began. The wholly religious character of the book was no drawback to its popularity, for the two great diaries of the time show how absolutely religion permeated the atmosphere surrounding both old and young.

Cotton Mather's diary gives various glimpses of his dealing with his own and other people's children. His son Increase, or "Cressy," as he was affectionately called, seems to have been particularly unresponsive to religious coercion. Mather's method, however, appears to have been more efficacious with the younger members of his family, and of Elizabeth and Samuel (seven years of age) he wrote: "My two younger children shall before the Psalm and prayer answer a Quæstion in the catechism; and have their Leaves ready turned unto the proofs of the Answer in the Bible; which they shall distinctly read unto us, and show what they prove. This also shall supply a fresh matter for prayer." Again he tells of his table talk: "Tho' I will have my table talk facetious as well as instructive . . . yett I will have the Exercise continually intermixed. I will set before them some sentence of the Bible, and make some useful Remarks upon it." Other people's children he taught as occasion offered; even when "on the Road in the Woods," he wrote on another day, "I, being desirous to do some Good, called some little children . . . and bestowed some Instruction with a little Book upon them." To children accustomed to instruction at all hours, the amusement found in the pages of the primer was far greater than in any other book printed in the colonies for years.

Certain titles indicate the nature of the meagre juvenile literary fare in the beginning of the new eighteenth century. In seventeen hundred Nicholas Boone, in his "Shop over against the old Meeting-house" in Boston, reprinted Janeway's "Token for Children." To this was added by the Boston printer a "Token for the children of New England, or some examples of children in whom the fear of God was remarkably budding when they dyed; in several parts of New England." Of course its author, the Reverend Mr. Mather, found colonial "examples" as deeply religious as any that the mother country could produce; but there is for us a grim humor in these various incidents concerning pious and precocious infants "of thin habit and pale countenance," whose pallor became that of death at so early an age. If it was by the repetition of such tales that the Puritan divine strove to convert Cressy, it may well be that the son considered it better policy, since Death claimed the little saints, to remain a sinner.

By seventeen hundred and six two juvenile books appeared from the press of Timothy Green in Boston. The first, "A Little Book for children wherein are set down several directions for little children: and several remarkable stories both ancient and modern of little children, divers whereof are lately deceased," was a reprint from an English book of the same title, and therefore has not in this chronicle the interest of the second book. The purpose of its publication is given in Mather's diary:

[1706] 22d. Im. Friday.

About this Time sending my little son to School, Where ye Child was Learning to Read, I did use every morning for diverse months, to Write in a plain Hand for the Child, and send thither by him, *a Lesson in Verse*, to be not only *read*, but also *Gott* by Heart. My proposal was to have the Child improve in goodness, at the same time that he improved in *Reading*. Upon further Thoughts I apprehended that a Collection of some of them would be serviceable to ye Good Education of other children. So I lett ye printer take them & print them, in some hope of some Help to thereby contributed unto that great Intention of a *Good Education*. The book is entituled *Good Lessons for Children;* or Instruction provided for a little Son to learn at School, when learning to Read.

Although this small book lives only by record, it is safe to assume from the extracts of the author's diary already quoted, that it lacked every quality of amusement, and was adapted only to those whom he described, in a sermon preached before the Governor and Council, as "verie Sharpe and early Ripe in their capacities." "Good Lessons" has the distinction of being the first American book to be composed, like many a modern publication, for a particular young child; and, with its purpose "to improve in goodness," struck clearly the keynote of the greater part of all writing for children during the succeeding one hundred and seventy-five years.

The first glimpse of the amusement book proper appears in that unique "History of Printing in America," by Isaiah

Thomas. This describes, among other old printers, one Thomas Fleet, who established himself in Boston about 1713. "At first," wrote Mr. Thomas, "he printed pamphlets for booksellers, small books for children and ballads" in Pudding Lane.* "He owned several negroes, one of which . . . was an ingenious man and cut on wooden blocks all the pictures which decorated the ballads and small books for his master."† As corroborative of these statements Thomas also mentions Thomas Fleet, Sr., as "the putative compiler of Mother Goose Melodies, which he first published in 1719, bearing the title of 'Songs for the Nursery.'"

Much discussion has arisen as to the earliest edition of Mother Goose. Thomas's suggestion as to the origin of the first American edition has been of late years relegated to the region of myth. Nevertheless, there is something to be said in favor of the existence of some book of nonsense at that time. The Boston "News Letter" for April 12–19, 1739, contained a criticism of Tate and Brady's version of the Psalms, in which the reviewer wrote that in Psalm VI the translators used the phrase, "a wretch forlorn." He added: "(1) There is nothing of this in the original or the English Psalter. (2) 'T is a low expression and to add a low one is the less allowable. But (3) what I am most concerned for is, that it will be apt to make our Children think of the line in their vulgar Play song; much like it, 'This is the maiden all forlorn.'" We recognize at once a reference to our nursery friend of the "House that Jack Built;" and if this and "Tom Thumb" were sold in Boston, why should not other ditties have been among the chap-books

* Thomas, *History of Printing in America*, vol. iii, p. 145. † *Ibid.*, vol. i, p. 294.

which Thomas remembered to have set up when a 'prentice lad in the printing-house of Zechariah Fowle, who in turn had copied some issued previously by Thomas Fleet? In further confirmation of Thomas's statement is a paragraph in the preface to an edition of Mother Goose, published in Boston in 1833, by Monroe & Francis. The editor traces the origin of these rhymes to a London book entitled, "Rhymes for the Nursery or Lullabies for Children," "that," he writes, "contained many of the identical pieces handed down to us." He continues: "The first book of the kind known to be printed in this country *bears* [*the italics are mine*] the title, '*Songs for the Nursery: or Mother Goose's Melodies for Children.*' Something probably intended to represent a goose, with a very long neck and mouth wide open, covered a large part of the title-page; at the bottom of which was: 'Printed by T. Fleet, at his printing house, Pudding Lane (Boston) 1719.' Several pages were missing, so that the whole number could not be ascertained." The editor clearly writes as if he had either seen, or heard accurately described, this piece of *Americana*, which the bibliophile to-day would consider a treasure trove. Later writers doubt whether any such book existed, for it is hardly credible that the Puritan element which so largely composed the population of Boston in the first quarter of the eighteenth century would have encouraged the printing of any nonsensical jingles.

Boston, however, was not at this time the only place in the colonies where primers and religious books were written and printed. In Philadelphia, Andrew Bradford, famous as the founder of the "American Weekly Mercury," had in 1714 put through his press, probably upon subscription, the

"Last Words and Dyeing Expressions of Hannah Hill, aged 11 years and near three Months." This morbid account of the death of a little Quakeress furnished the Philadelphia children with a book very similar to Mather's "Token." Not to be outdone by any precocious example in Pennsylvania, the Reverend Mr. Mather soon found an instance of "Early Piety in Elizabeth Butcher of Boston, being just 8 years and 11 months old," when she died in 1718. In two years two editions of her life had been issued "to instruct and to invite little children to the exercise of early piety."

Such mortuary effusions were so common at the time that Benjamin Franklin's witty skit upon them is apropos in this connection. In 1719, at the age of sixteen, under the pseudonym of Mrs. Dogood, he wrote a series of letters for his brother's paper, "The New England Courant." From the following extract, taken from these letters, it is evident that these children's "Last Words" followed the prevailing fashion:

A Receipt to make a *New England*
Funeral *Elegy*.

For the title of your Elegy. Of these you may have enough ready made at your Hands: But if you should chuse to make it yourself you must be sure not to omit the Words *Aetatis Suae*, which will beautify it exceedingly.

For the subject of your Elegy. Take one of your neighbors who has lately departed this life; it is no great matter at what age the Party Dy'd, but it will be best if he went away suddenly, being *Kill'd*, *Drown'd* or *Froze to Death*.

Having chosen the Person, take all his Virtues, Excellencies, &c. and if he have not enough, you may borrow some to make up a sufficient Quantity: To these add his last Words, dying Expressions, &c. if they are to be had: mix all these together, and be sure you strain them well. Then season all with a Handful or two of Melancholy Expressions, such as *Dreadful*, *Dreadly*, *cruel*, *cold*, *Death*, *unhappy*, *Fate*, *weeping Eyes*, &c. Having mixed all these Ingredients well, put them in an empty Scull of some *young Harvard;* (but in case you have ne'er a One at Hand, you may use your *own*,) then let them Ferment for the Space of a Fortnight, and by that Time they will be incorporated into a Body, which take out and having prepared a sufficient Quantity of double Rhimes, such as *Power*, *Flower;* *Quiver*, *Shiver;* *Grieve us*, *Leave us;* *tell you*, *excel you;* *Expeditions*, *Physicians;* *Fatigue him*, *Intrigue him;* &c. you must spread all upon Paper, and if you can procure a Scrap of Latin to put at the *End*, it will garnish it mightily: then having affixed your Name at the bottom with a *Maestus Composuit*, you will have an Excellent Elegy.

N.B. This Receipt will serve when a Female is the subject of your Elegy, provided you borrow a greater Quantity of Virtues, Excellencies &c.

Of other original books for children of colonial parents in the first quarter of that century, "A Looking-glass" did but mirror more religious episodes concerning infants, while Mather in his zeal had also published "An Earnest Exhortation" to New England children, and "The A, B, C, of religion. Fitted unto the youngest and lowest capacities." To this, taking advantage of the use of rhymes, he appended further instruction, including "The Body of Divinity versified." With our knowledge of the clergyman's methods with his congregation it is not difficult to imagine that he insisted upon the purchase of these godly aids for every household.

In attempting to reproduce the conditions of family life in the early settlements and towns of colonial days, we turn quite naturally to the newspapers, whose appearance in the first quarter of the eighteenth century was gladly welcomed by the people of their time, and whose files are now eagerly searched for items of great or small importance. Indeed, much information can be gathered from their advertisements, which often filled the major part of these periodicals. Apparently shop-keepers were keen to take advantage of such space as was reserved for them, as sometimes a marginal note informed the public that other advertisements must wait for the next issue to appear.

Booksellers' announcements, however, are not too frequent in Boston papers, and are noticeably lacking in the early issues of the Philadelphia "Weekly Mercury." This dearth of book-news accounts for the difficulty experienced by book-lovers of that town in procuring literature—a lack noticed at once by the wide-awake young Franklin upon his arrival in the city, and recorded in his biography as follows:

"At the time I established myself in Pennsylvania [1728] there was not a bookseller's shop in any of the colonies to the southward of Boston. In New York and Phil'a. the printers were indeed stationers; they sold only paper, etc., ballads, and a few books. Those who lov'd reading were obliged to send for their books from London."

Franklin undertook to better this condition by opening

a shop for the sale of foreign books. Both he and his rival in journalism, Andrew Bradford, had stationer's shops, in which were to be had besides "Good Writing Paper; Cyphering Slates; Ink Powders, etc., Chapmens Books and Ballads." Bradford also advertised in seventeen hundred and thirty that all persons could be supplied with "Primers and small Histories of many sorts." "Small histories" were probably chap-books, which, hawked about the country by peddlers or chapmen, contained tales of "Fair Rosamond," "Jane Grey," "Tom Thumb" or "Tom Hick-a-Thrift," and though read by old and young, were hardly more suitable for juvenile reading than the religious elegies then so popular. These chap-books were sold in considerable quantities on account of their cheapness, and included religious subjects as well as tales of adventure.

One of the earliest examples of this chap-book literature, thought suitable for children, was printed in the colonies by the press of Thomas Fleet, already mentioned as a printer of small books. This book of 1736, being intended for ready sale, was such as every Puritan would buy for the family library. Entitled "The Prodigal Daughter," it told in Psalm-book metre of a "proud, vain girl, who, because her parents would not indulge her in all her extravagances, bargained with the devil to poisen them." The parents, however, were warned by an angel of her intentions:

"One night her parents sleeping were in bed
Nothing but troubled dreams run in their head,
At length an angel did to them appear
Saying awake, and unto me give ear.

A meſſenger I'm sent by Heaven kind
To let you know your lives are both deſign'd;
Your graceleſs child, whom you love ſo dear,
She for your precious lives hath laid a ſnare.
To poiſon you the devil tempts her ſo,
She hath no power from the ſnare to go:
But God ſuch care doth of his ſervants take,
Thoſe that believe on Him He 'll not forſake.

"You muſt not uſe her cruel or ſevere,
For though theſe things to you I do declare,
It is to ſhow you what the Lord can do,
He ſoon can turn her heart, you 'll find it ſo."

The daughter, discovered in her attempt to poison their food, was reproached by the mother for her evil intention and swooned. Every effort failed to "bring her spirits to revive:"

"Four days they kept her, when they did prepare
To lay her body in the duſt we hear,
At her funeral a ſermon then was preach'd,
All other wicked children for to teach. . . .
But ſuddenly they bitter groans did hear
Which much ſurprized all that then were there.
At length they did obſerve the diſmal ſound
Came from the body juſt laid in the ground."

The Puritan pride in funeral display is naïvely exhibited in the portrayal of the girl when she "in her coffin sat, and did admire her winding sheet," before she related her experiences "among lonesome wild deſerts and briary woods, which diſmal were and dark." But immediately after her description of the lake of burning misery and of the fierce grim Tempter, the Puritan matter-of-fact acceptance of it all is suggested by the concluding lines:

"When thus her ſtory ſhe to them had told,
She ſaid, put me to bed for I am cold."

The illustrations of a later edition entered thoroughly into the spirit of the author's intent. The contemporary opinion of the French character is quaintly shown in the portrait of the Devil dressed as a French gentleman, his cloven foot discovering his identity. Whatever deficiencies are revealed in these early attempts to illustrate, they invariably expressed the artist's purpose, and in this case the Devil, after the girl's conversion, is drawn in lines very acceptable to Puritan children's idea of his personality.

Almanacs also were in demand, and furnished parents and children, in many cases, with their entire library for week-day reading. "Successive numbers hung from a string by the chimney or ranked by years and generations on cupboard shelves."* But when Franklin made "Poor Richard" an international success, he, by giving short extracts from Swift, Steele, Defoe, and Bacon, accustomed the provincial population, old and young, to something better than the meagre religious fare provided by the colonial press.

Such, then, were the literary conditions for children when an advertisement inserted in the "Weekly Mercury" gave promise of better days for the little Philadelphians.† Strangely enough, this attempt to make learning seem attractive to children did not appear in the booksellers' lists; but crowded in between Tandums, Holland Tapes, London Steel, and

* Sears, *American Literature*, p. 86.

†Although this appears to be the first advertisement of gilt horn-books in Philadelphia papers, an inventory of the estate of Michael Perry, a Boston bookseller, made in seventeen hundred, includes sixteen dozen gilt horn-books.

The Devil appears as a French Gentleman

good Muscavado Sugar,—"Guilt horn books" were advertised by Joseph Sims in 1740 as "for sale on reasonable Terms for Cash."

Horn-books in themselves were only too common, and not in the least delightful. Made of thin wood, whereon was placed a printed sheet of paper containing the alphabet and Lord's Prayer, a horn-book was hardly, properly speaking, a book at all. But when the printed page was covered with yellowish transparent horn, secured to the wooden back by strips of brass, it furnished an economical and practically indestructible elementary text-book for thousands of English-speaking children on both sides of the Atlantic. Sometimes an effort was also made to guard against the inconvenient faculty of children for losing school-books, by attaching a cord, which, passing through a hole in the handle of the board, was hung around the scholar's neck. But since nothing is proof against the ingenuity of a schoolboy, many were successfully disposed of. Although printed by thousands, few in England or in America have survived the century that has elapsed since they were used. Occasionally, in tearing down an old building, one of these horn-books has been found; dropped in a convenient hole, it has remained secure from parents' sight, until brought to light by workmen and prized as a curiosity by grown people of the present generation. This notice of little gilt horn-books was inserted in the "Weekly Mercury" but once. Whether the supply was quickly exhausted, or whether they did not prove a successful novelty, can never be known; but at least they herald the approach of the little gilt story-books which ten years later were to make the name of John Newbery well known in English households, and hardly less familiar in the American colonies.

So far the only attractions to induce children to read have been through the pictures in the Primer of New England, and by the gilding of the horn-book. From further south comes the first note of amusement in reading, as well as the first expression of pleasure from the children themselves in regard to a book. In 1741, in Virginia, two letters were written and received by R. H. Lee and George Washington. These letters, which afford the first in any way authentic account of tales of real entertainment, are given by Mr. Lossing in "The Home of Washington," and tell their own tale:

[*Richard Henry Lee to George Washington*]

Pa brought me two pretty books full of pictures he got them in Alexandria they have pictures of dogs and cats and tigers and elefants and ever so many pretty things cousin bids me send you one of them it has a picture of an elefant and a little indian boy on his back like uncle jo's Sam pa says if I learn my tasks good he will let uncle jo bring me to see you will you ask your ma to let you come to see me.

Richard henry Lee.

[*G. Washington to R. H. Lee*]

Dear Dickey—I thank you very much for the pretty picture book you gave me. Sam asked me to show him the pictures and I showed him all the pictures in it; and I read to him how the tame Elephant took care of the Master's little boy, and put him on his back and would not let anybody touch his master's little son. I can read three or four pages sometimes without missing a word. . . . I have a little piece of poetry about the picture book you gave me but I mustn't tell you who wrote the poetry.

> G. W.'s compliments to R. H. L.
> And likes his book full well,
> Henceforth will count him his friend
> And hopes many happy days he may spend.

Your good friend
GEORGE WASHINGTON.

In a note Mr. Lossing states that he had copies of these two letters, sent him by a Mr. Lee, who wrote: "The letter of Richard Henry Lee was written by himself, and uncorrected sent by him to his boy friend George Washington. The poetical effusion was, I have heard, written by a Mr. Howard, a gentleman who used to visit at the house of Mr. Washington."

It would be gratifying to know the titles of these two books, so evidently English chap-book tales. It is probable that they were imported by a shop-keeper in Alexandria, as in seventeen hundred and forty-one there was only one press in Virginia, owned by William Sharps, who had moved from Annapolis in seventeen hundred and thirty-six. Luxuries were so much more common among the Virginia planters, and life was so much more roseate in hue than was the case in the northern colonies, that it seems most natural that two southern boys should have left the earliest account of any real story-books. Though unfortunately nameless, they at least form an interesting coincidence. Bought in seventeen hundred and forty-one, they follow just one hundred years later than the meeting of the General Court, which was responsible for the preparation of Cotton's "Milk for Babes," and precede by a century the date when an American story-book literature was recognized as very different from that written for English children.

CHAPTER II

1747–1767

He who learns his letters fair,
Shall have a coach and take the air.

Royal Primer, Newbery, 1762

Our king the good
No man of blood.

The New England Primer, 1762

CHAPTER II

1747–1767

The Play-Book in England

THE vast horde of story-books so constantly poured into modern nurseries makes it difficult to realize that the library of the early colonial child consisted of such books as have been already described. The juvenile books to-day are multiform. The quantities displayed upon shop-counters or ranged upon play-room shelves include a variety of subjects bewildering to all but those whose business necessitates a knowledge of this kind of literature. For the little child there is no lack of gayly colored pictures and short tales in large print; for the older boys and girls there lies a generous choice, ranging from Bunny stories to Jungle Books, or they

> "May see how all things are,
> Seas and cities near and far.
> And the flying fairies' looks
> In the picture story-books."

The contrast is indeed extreme between that scanty fare of dull sermons and "The New England Primer" given to the little people of the early eighteenth century, and this superabundance prepared with lavish care for the nation of American children.

The beginning of this complex juvenile literature is, therefore, to be regarded as a comparatively modern invention of about seventeen hundred and forty-five. From that date can be traced the slow growth of a literature written with an avowed intention of furnishing amusement as well as instruction; and in the toy-books published one hundred and fifty years ago are found the prototypes of the present modes of bringing fun and knowledge to the American fireside.

The question at once arises as to the reason why this literature came into existence; why was it that children after seventeen hundred and fifty should have been favored in a way unknown to their parents?

To even the casual reader of English literature the answer is plain, if this subject of toy-books be regarded as of near kin to the larger body of writing. It has been somewhat the custom to consider children's literature as a thing wholly apart from that of adults, probably because the majority of the authors of these little tales have so generally lacked the qualities indispensable for any true literary work. In reality the connection between the two is somewhat like that of parent and child; the smaller body, though lacking in power, has closely imitated the larger mass of writing in form and kind, and has reflected, sometimes clearly, sometimes dimly, the good or bad fashions that have shared the successive periods of literary history, like a child who unconsciously reproduces a parent's foibles or excellences.

It is to England, then, that we must look to find the conditions out of which grew the necessity for this modern invention—the story-book.

The love of stories has been the splendid birthright of every child in all ages and in all lands. "Stories," wrote Thackeray,—"stories exist everywhere; there is no calculating the distance through which the stories have come to us, the number of languages through which they have been filtered, or the centuries during which they have been told. Many of them have been narrated almost in their present shape for thousands of years to the little copper-coloured Sanscrit children, listening to their mothers under the palm-trees by the banks of the yellow Jumna—their Brahmin mother, who softly narrated them through the ring in her nose. The very same tale has been heard by the Northern Vikings as they lay on their shields on deck; and the Arabs couched under the stars on the Syrian plains when their flocks were gathered in, and their mares were picketed by the tents." This picturesque description leads exactly to the point to be emphasized: that children shared in the simple tales of their people as long as those tales retained their freshness and simplicity; but when, as in England in the eighteenth century, the literature lost these qualities and became artificial, critical, and even skeptical, it lost its charm for the little ones and they no longer cared to listen to it.

Fashion and taste were then alike absorbed in the works of Dryden, Pope, Addison, Steele, and Swift, and the novels from the pens of Richardson, Fielding, and Smollett had begun to claim and to hold the attention of the English reading public. The children, however, could neither comprehend nor enjoy the witty criticism and subtle treatment of the topics discussed by the older men, although, as will be seen in another chapter, the novels became, in both the original and in the abridged forms, the delight of many a "young master and miss." Meanwhile, in the American colonies the people who could afford to buy books inherited their taste for literature as well as for tea from the Puritans and fashionables in the mother country; although it is a fact familiar to all, that the works of the comparatively few native authors lagged, in spirit and in style, far behind the writings of Englishmen of the time.

The reading of one who was a boy in the older era of the urbane Addison and the witty Pope, and a man in the newer period of the novelists, is well described in Benjamin Franklin's autobiography. "All the little money," wrote that book-lover, "that came into my hands was laid out in books. Pleased with the Pilgrim's Progress, my collection was of John Bunyan's works in separate volumes. I afterwards sold them to buy R. Burton's Historical Collections; they were Chapmen's books, and cheap, 40 or 50 in all."

Burton's "Historical Collections" contained history, travels, adventures, fiction, natural history, and biography. So great was the favor in which they were held in the eighteenth century that the compiler, Nathaniel Crouch, almost lost his identity in his pseudonym, and like the late Mr. Clemens, was better known by his nom-de-plume than by his family name. According to Dunton, he "melted down the best of the English histories into twelve-penny books, which are filled with wonders, rarities and curiosities." Although characterized by Dr. Johnson as "very proper to allure backward readers," the contents of many of the various books afforded the knowledge and entertainment eagerly grasped by Franklin and other future makers of the American nation. The scarcity of historical works concerning the colonies made Burton's account of the "English Empire in America" at once a mine of interest to wide-awake boys of the day.

Number VIII, entitled "Winter Evenings' Entertainment," was long a source of amusement with its stories and riddles, and its title was handed down to other books of a similar nature. To children, however, the best-known volume of the series was Burton's illustrated versification of Bible stories called "The Youth's Divine Pastime." But the subjects chosen by Burton were such as belonged to a very plain-spoken age; and as the versifier was no euphuist in his relation of facts, the result was a remarkable "Pastime for Youth." The literature read by English children was, of course, the same; the little ones of both countries ate of the same tree of knowledge of facts, often either silly or revolting.

To deliver the younger and future generations from such unpalatable and indigestible mental food, there was soon to appear in London a man, John Newbery by name, who, already a printer, publisher, and vendor of patent medicines, seized the opportunity to issue stories written especially for the amusement of little children.

While Newbery was making his plans to provide pleasure for young folks in England, in the colonies the idea of a child's need of recreation through books was slowly gaining ground. It is well to note the manner in which the little colonists were prepared to receive Newbery's books as recreative features crept gradually into the very few publications of which there is record.

In seventeen hundred and forty-five native talent was still entirely confined to writing for little people lugubrious sermons or discourses delivered on Sunday and "Catechize days," and afterwards printed for larger circulation. The reprints from

English publications were such exotics as, "A Poesie out of Mr. Dod's Garden," an alluring title, which did not in the least deceive the small colonials as to the religious nature of its contents.

In New York the Dutch element, until the advent of Garrat Noel, paid so little attention to the subject of juvenile literature that the popularity of Watts's "Divine Songs" (issued by an Englishman) is well attested by the fact that at present it is one of the very few child's books of any kind recorded as printed in that city before 1760. But in Boston, old Thomas Fleet, in 1741, saw the value of the element of some entertainment in connection with reading, and, when he published "The Parents' Gift, containing a choice collection of God's judgments and Mercies," lives of the Evangelists, and other religious matter, he added a "variety of pleasant Pictures proper for the Entertainment of Children." This is, perhaps, the first printed acknowledgment in America that pictures were commendable to parents *because* entertaining to their offspring. Such an idea put into words upon paper and advertised in so well-read a sheet as the "Boston Evening Post," must surely have impressed fathers and mothers really solicitous for the family welfare and anxious to provide harmless pleasure. This pictorial element was further encouraged by Franklin, when, in 1747, he reprinted, probably for the first time in this country, "Dilworth's New Guide to the English Tongue." In this school-book, after the alphabets and spelling lessons, a special feature was introduced, that is, illustrated "Select Fables." The cuts at the top of each fable possess an added interest from the supposition that they were engraved by the printer himself; and the constant use of the "Guide" by colonial school-masters and mistresses made their pupils unconsciously quite ready for more illustrated and fewer homiletic volumes.

Indeed, before the middle of the century pictures had become an accepted feature of the few juvenile books, and "The History of the Holy Jesus" versified for little ones was issued by at least two old Boston printers in 1747 and 1748 with more than a dozen cuts. Among the rare extant copies of this small chap-book is one that, although torn and disfigured by tiny fingers and the century and a half since it pleased its first owner, bears the personal touch of this inscription: "Ebenezer ... Bought June ... 1749 ... price o = 2 = d." Was the price marked upon its page as a reminder that two shillings was a large price to pay for a boy's book? Perhaps for this reason it received the careful handling that has enabled us to examine it, when so many of its contemporaries and successors have vanished.

The versified story, notwithstanding its quaintness of diction, begins with a dignified directness:

> "The glorious blessed Time had come,
> The Father had decreed,
> Jesus of *Mary* there was born,
> And in a Manger laid."

At the end are two *Hymns*, entitled "Delight in the Lord Jesus," and "Absence from Christ intolerable." The final stanza is typical of one Puritan doctrine:

> "The Devil throws his fiery Darts,
> And wicked Ones do act their parts,

To ruin me when Christ is gone,
And leaves me all alone."

The woodcuts are not the least interesting feature of this old-time duodecimo, from the picture showing the mother reading to her children to the illustration of the quaking of the earth on the day of the crucifixion. Crude and badly drawn as they now seem, they were surely sufficient to attract the child of their generation.

About the same time old Zechariah Fowle, who apprenticed Isaiah Thomas, and both printed and vended chap-books in Back Street, Boston, advertised among his list of books "Lately Publish'd" this same small book, together with "A Token for Youth," the "Life and Death of Elizabeth Butcher," "A Preservative from the Sins and Follies of Childhood and Youth," "The Prodigal Daughter," "The Happy Child," and "The New Gift for Children with Cuts." Of these "The New Gift" was certainly a real story-book, as one of a later edition still extant readily proves.

Thus the children in both countries were prepared to enjoy Newbery's miniature story-books, although for somewhat different reasons: in England the literature had reached a point too artificial to be interesting to little ones; in America the product of the press and the character of the majority of the juvenile importations, the reprints, or home-made chap-books, has been shown to be such as would hardly attract those who were to be the future arbiters of the colonies' destiny.

The reasons for the coming to light of this new form of infant literature have been dwelt upon in order to show the necessity for some change in the kind of reading-matter to be put in the hands of the younger members of the family. The natural order of consideration is next to point out the phase it assumed upon its appearance in England,—a phase largely due to the influence of one man,—and once there, the modifications effected by the fashions in adult fiction.

Although there was already much interest in the education and welfare of children still in the nursery, the character of the first play-books was probably due to the esteem in which the opinions of the philosopher, John Locke, were held. He it was who gradually moved the vane of public opinion around to serious consideration of recreation as a factor in the well-being of these nursery inmates. Although it took time for Locke's ideas upon the subject to sink into the public mind, it is impossible to compare one of the first attempts to produce a play-book, "The Child's New Play-thing," with the advice written to his friend, Edward Clarke, without feeling that the progress from the religious books to primers and readers (such as "Dilworth's Guide"), and then onward to story-books, was largely the result of the publication of his letters under the title of "Thoughts on Education."

In these letters Locke took an extraordinary course: he first made a quaint plea for the *general welfare* of Mr. Clarke's little son. "I imagine," he wrote, "the minds of children are as easily turned this or that way as Water itself, and though this be the principal Part, and our main Care should be about the inside, yet the Clay Cottage is not to be neglected. I shall therefore begin with the case, and consider first the *Health* of the body." Under Health he discussed clothing, including thin shoes, "that they may leak and let in Water." A pause was then made to show the benefits of wet feet as against the apparent disadvantages of filthy stockings and muddy boots; for mothers even in that time were inclined to consider their floors and steps. Bathing next received attention. Bathing every day in cold water, Locke regarded as exceedingly desirable; no exceptions were to be made, even in the case of a "puleing and tender" child. The beneficial effects of air, sunlight, the establishment of good conduct, diet, sleep, and "physick" were all discussed by the doctor and philosopher, before the development of the mind was touched upon. "Education," he wrote, "concerns itself with the forming of Children's Minds, giving them that seasoning early, which shall influence their Lives later." This seasoning referred to the training of children in matters pertaining to their general government and to the reverence of parents. For the Puritan population it was undoubtedly a shock to find Locke interesting himself in, and moreover advocating, dancing as a part of a child's education; and worst of all, that he should mention it before their hobby, LEARNING. In this connection it is worth while to make mention of a favorite primer, which, published about the middle of the eighteenth century, was entitled "The Hobby Horse." Locke was quite aware that his method would be criticised, and therefore took the bull by the horns in the following manner. He admitted that to put the subject of learning last was a cause for wonder, "especially if I tell you I think it the least part. This may seem strange in the mouth of a bookish man, and this making usually the chief, if not only bustle and stir about children; this being almost that alone, which is thought on, when People talk about Education, make it the greater Paradox." An unusual piece of advice it most surely was to parents to whose children came the task of learning to read as soon as they were given spoon-food.

Even more revolutionary to the custom of an eighteenth century mother was the admonition that reading "be never made a Task." Locke, however, was not the man to urge a cure for a bad habit without prescribing a remedy, so he went on to say that it was always his "Fancy that Learning be made a Play and Recreation to Children"—a "Fancy" at present much in vogue. To accomplish this desirable result, "Dice and Play-things with the Letters on them" were recommended to teach children the alphabet; "and," he added, "twenty other ways may be found . . . to make this kind of Learning a Sport to them." Letter-blocks were in this way made popular, and formed the approved and advanced method until in these latter days pedagogy has swept aside the letter-blocks and syllabariums and carried the sport to word-pictures.

This theory had a practical result in the introduction to many households of "The Child's New Play-thing." This book, already mentioned, was printed in England in seventeen hundred and forty-three, and dedicated to Prince George. In seventeen hundred and forty-four we find through the "Boston Evening Post" of January 23 that the third edition was sold by Joseph Edwards, in Cornhill, and it was probably from this edition that the first American edition was printed in seventeen hundred and fifty. From the following description of this American reprint (one of which is happily in the Lenox Collection), it will be seen that the "Play-thing" was an attempt to follow Locke's advice, as well as a connecting link between the primer of the past and the story-book of the near future.

The title, which the illustration shows, reads, "The Child's New Play-thing being a spelling-book intended to make Learning to read a diversion instead of a task. Consisting of Scripture-histories, fables, stories, moral and religious precepts, proverbs, songs, riddles, dialogues, &c. The whole adapted to the capacities of children, and divided into lessons of one, two, three and four syllables. The fourth edition. To which is added three dialogues; 1. Shewing how a little boy shall make every body love him. 2. How a little boy shall grow wiser than the rest of his school-fellows. 3. How a little boy shall become a great man. Designed for the use of schools, or for children before they go to school."

Coverless and faded, hard usage is written in unmistakable characters upon this play-thing of a whole family. Upon a fly-leaf are the autographs of "Ebenezer Ware and Sarah Ware, Their Book," and upon another page these two names with the addition of the signatures of "Ichabod Ware and Cyrus Ware 1787." One parent may have used it when it was fresh from the press of Draper & Edwards in Boston; then, through enforced economy, handed it down to the next generation, who doubtless scorned the dedication so eminently proper in seventeen hundred and fifty, so thoroughly out of place thirty-seven years later. There it stands in large black type:

To his ROYAL HIGHNESS PRINCE GEORGE This Little Play-thing is most humbly dedicated
By
His ROYAL HIGHNESS'S
Devoted Servant

THE

Child's new Play-Thing:

BEING A

SPELLING-BOOK

INTENDED

To make the Learning to *Read* a *Diversion* instead of a *Task*.

Consisting of

Scripture-Histories, Fables, Stories, Moral and Religious Precepts, Proverbs, Songs, Riddles, Dialogues, &c.

The Whole adapted to the Capacities of Children, and Divided into Lessons of one, two, three and four Syllables.

The FOURTH EDITION.

To which is added Three Dialogues:

1. Shewing how a little Boy shall make every body love him. 2. How a little Boy shall grow wiser than the rest of his School-fellows. 3. How a little Boy shall become a great Man.

Designed for the USE of SCHOOLS, or for Children before they go to School

---

BOSTON: Printed by J. DRAPER. J. EDWARDS in Cornhill.

Title-page from "The Child's new Play-Thing"

Of especial interest are the alphabets in "Roman, Italian, and English Names" on the third page, while page four contains the dear old alphabet in rhyme, fortunately not altogether forgotten in this prosaic age. We recognize it as soon as we see it.

"A Apple-Pye
B bit it
C cut it,"

and involuntarily add, D divided it. After the spelling lessons came fables, proverbs, and the splendid "Stories proper to raise the Attention and excite the Curiosity of Children" of any age; namely, "St. George and the Dragon," "Fortunatus," "Guy of Warwick," "Brother and Sister," "Reynard the Fox," "The Wolf and the Kid." "The Good Dr. Watts," writes Mrs. Field, "is supposed to have had a hand in the composition of this toy book especially in the stories, one of which is quite in the style of the old hymn writer." Here it is:

"Once on a time two dogs went out to walk. Tray was a good dog, and would not hurt the least thing in the world, but Snap was cross, and would snarl and bite at all that came in his way. At last they came to a town. All the dogs came round them. Tray hurt none of them, but Snap would grin at one, snarl at the next, and bite a third, till at last they fell on him and tore him limb from limb, and as poor Tray was with him, he met with his death at the same time.

Moral

"By this fable you see how dangerous it is to be in company with bad boys. Tray was a quiet harmless dog, and hurt nobody, but, &c."*

* Field, *The Child and his Book*, p. 223.

Thus we find that Locke sowed the seed, Watts watered the soil in which the seed fell, and that Newbery, after mixing in ideas from his very fertile brain, soon reaped a golden harvest from the crop of readers, picture-books, and little histories which he, with the aid of certain well-known authors, produced.

According to his biographer, Mr. Charles Welsh, John Newbery was born in a quaint parish of England in seventeen hundred and thirteen. Although his father was only a small farmer, Newbury inherited his bookish tastes from an ancestor, Ralph or Rafe Newbery, who had been a great publisher of the sixteenth century. Showing no inclination toward the life of a farmer, the boy, at sixteen, had already entered the shop of a merchant in Reading. The name of this merchant is not known, but inference points to Mr. Carnan, printer, proprietor, and editor of one of the earliest provincial newspapers. In seventeen hundred and thirty-seven, at the death of Carnan, John Newbery, then about twenty-four years of age, found himself one of the proprietor's heirs and an executor of the estate. Carnan left a widow, to whom, to quote her son, Newbery's "love of books and acquirements as a printer rendered him very acceptable." The amiable and well-to-do widow and Newbery were soon married, and their youngest son, Francis Newbery, eventually succeeded his father in the business of publishing.

Shortly after Newbery's marriage his ambition and enterprise resulted in the establishment of his family in London, where, in seventeen hundred and forty-four, he opened a warehouse at *The Bible and Crown*, near Devereux Court, without

A LITTLE PRETTY
POCKET-BOOK,
INTENDED FOR THE
INSTRUCTION and AMUSEMENT
OF
LITTLE MASTER TOMMY,
AND
PRETTY MISS POLLY.
With Two LETTERS from
JACK the GIANT-KILLER
AS ALSO
A BALL and PINCUSHION;
The Use of which will infallibly make TOMMY a good Boy, and POLLY a good Girl.
To which is added,
A LITTLE SONG-BOOK,
BEING
A NEW ATTEMPT to teach CHILDREN the Use of the English Alphabet, by Way of Diversion.

THE FIRST *WORCESTER* EDITION.

PRINTED at WORCESTER, *Massachusetts*.
By ISAIAH THOMAS,
And SOLD, Wholesale and Retail, at his Book-Store. MDCCLXXXVII.

Title-page from "A Little Pretty Pocket-Book"

Temple Bar. Meanwhile he had associated himself with Benjamin Collins, a printer in Salisbury. Collins both planned and printed some of Newbery's toy volumes, and his name likewise was well-known to shop-keepers in the colonies. Newbery soon found that his business warranted another move nearer to the centre of trade. He therefore combined two establishments into one at the now celebrated corner of St. Paul's Churchyard, and at the same time decided to confine his attention exclusively to book publishing and medicine vending.

Before his departure from Devereux Court, Newbery had published at least one book for juvenile readers. The title reads: "Little Pretty Pocket-Book, intended for the instruction and Amusement of Little Master Tommy and Pretty Miss Polly, with an agreeable Letter to read from Jack the Giant Killer, as also a Ball and Pincushion, the use of which will infallibly make Tommy a good Boy, and Polly a good Girl. To the whole is prefixed a letter on education humbly addressed to all Parents, Guardians, Governesses, &c., wherein rules are laid down for making their children strong, healthy, virtuous, wise and happy." To this extraordinarily long title were added couplets from Dryden and Pope, probably because extracts from these poets were usually placed upon the title-page of books for grown people; possibly also in order to give a finish to miniature volumes that would be like the larger publications. A wholly simple method of writing title-pages never came into even Newbery's original mind; he did for the juvenile customer exactly what he was accustomed to do for his father and mother. And yet the habit of spreading out over the page the entire contents of the book was not without value: it gave the purchaser no excuse for not knowing what was to be found within its covers; and in the days when books were a luxury and literary reviews non-existent, the country trade was enabled to make a better choice.

The manner in which the "Little Pretty Pocket-Book" is written is so characteristic of those who were the first to attempt to write for the younger generation in an amusing way, that it is worth while to examine briefly the topics treated. An American reprint of a later date, now in the Lenox Collection, will serve to show the method chosen to combine instruction with amusement. The book itself is miniature in size, about two by four inches, with embossed gilt paper covers—Newbery's own specialty as a binding. The sixty-five little illustrations at the top of its pages were numerous enough to afford pleasure to any eighteenth century child, although they were crude in execution and especially lacked true perspective. The first chapter after the "Address to Parents" and to the other people mentioned on the title-page gives letters to Master Tommy and Miss Polly. First, Tommy is congratulated upon the good character that his Nurse has given him, and instructed as to the use of the "Pocket-Book," "which will teach you to play at all those innocent games that good Boys and Girls divert themselves with." The boy reader is next advised to mark his good and bad actions with pins upon a red and black ball. Little Polly is then given similar congratulations and instructions, except that in her case a pincushion is to be substituted for a ball. Then follow thirty pages devoted to "alphabetically digested" games, from "The *great A Play*" and "The *Little*

98 RULES *for* BEHAVIOUR.

BEHAVIOUR *when at* HOME.

1 MAKE a Bow always when you come Home, and be inſtantly uncovered.

2 Be never covered at Home, eſpecially before thy Parents or Strangers.

3 Never ſet in the Preſence of thy Parents without bidding, though no Stranger be preſent.

A page from "A Little Pretty Pocket-Book"

a Play" to "The *great and little Rs*," when plays, or the author's imagination, give out and rhymes begin the alphabet anew. Modern picture alphabets have not improved much upon this jingle:

> "Great A, B and C
> And tumble down D,
> The Cat 's a blind buff,
> And she cannot see."

Next in order are four fables with morals (written in the guise of letters), for in Newbery's books and in those of a much later period, we feel, as Mr. Welsh writes, a "strong determination on the part of the authors to place the moral plainly in sight and to point steadily to it." Pictures also take a leading part in this effort to inculcate good behaviour; thus *Good Children* are portrayed in cuts, which accompany the directions for attaining perfection. Proverbs, having been hitherto introduced into school-books, appear again quite naturally in this source of diversion, which closes—at least in the American edition—with sixty-three "Rules for Behaviour." These rules include those suitable for various occasions, such as "At the Meeting-House," "Home," "The Table," "In Company," and "When abroad with other Children." To-day, when many such rules are as obsolete as the tiny pages themselves, this chapter affords many glimpses of the customs and etiquette of the old-fashioned child's life. Such a direction as "Be not hasty to run out of Meeting-House when Worship is ended, as if thou weary of being there" (probably an American adaptation of the English original), recalls the well-filled colonial meeting-house, where weary children sat for hours on high seats, with dangling legs, or screwed their small bodies in vain efforts to touch the floor. Again we can see the anxious mothers, when, after the long sermon was brought to a close, they put restraining hands upon the little ones, lest they, in haste to be gone, should forget this admonition. The formalism of the time is suggested in this request, "Make a Bow always when come Home, and be instantly uncovered," for the ceremony of polite manners in these bustling days has so much relaxed that the modern boy does all that is required if he remembers to be "instantly uncovered when come Home." Among the numerous other requirements only one more may be cited—a rule which reveals the table manners of polite society in its requisite for genteel conduct: "Throw not anything under the Table. Pick not thy teeth at the Table, unless holding thy Napkin before thy mouth with thine other Hand." With such an array of intellectual and moral contents, the little "Pocket-Book" may appear to-day to be almost anything except an amusement book. Yet this was the phase that the English play-book first assumed, and it must not be forgotten that English prose fiction was only then coming into existence, except such germs as are found in the character sketches in the "Spectator" and in the cleverly told incidents by Defoe.

In 1744, when Newbery published this duodecimo, Dr. Samuel Johnson was the presiding genius of English letters; four years earlier, fiction had come prominently into the foreground with the publication of "Pamela" by Samuel Richardson; and between seventeen hundred and forty and seventeen hundred and fifty-two, Richardson's "Clarissa

Harlowe," Smollett's "Roderick Random" and "Peregrine Pickle," and Fielding's "Tom Jones" were published. This fact may seem irrelevant to the present subject; nevertheless, the idea of a veritable story-book, that is a book relating a tale, does not seem to have entered Newbery's mind until after these novels had met with a deserved and popular success.

The result of Newbery's first efforts to follow Locke's advice was so satisfactory that his wares were sought most eagerly. "Very soon," said his son, Francis Newbery, "he was in the full employment of his talents in writing and publishing books of amusement and instruction for Children. The call for them was immense, an edition of many thousands being sometimes exhausted during the Christmas holidays. His friend, Dr. Samuel Johnson, who, like other grave characters, could now and then be jocose, had used to say of him, 'Newbery is an extraordinary man, for I know not whether he has read or written most Books.'"*

The bookseller was no less clever in his use of other people's wits. No one knows how many of the tiny gilt bindings covered stories told by impecunious writers, to whom the proceeds in times of starvation were bread if not butter. Newbery, though called by Goldsmith "the philanthropic publisher of St. Paul's Churchyard," knew very well the worth to his own pocket of these authors' skill in story-writing. Between the years seventeen hundred and fifty-seven and seventeen hundred and sixty-seven, the English publisher was at the height of his prosperity; his name became

* Welsh, *Bookseller of the Last Century*, pp. 22, 23.

a household word in England, and was hardly less well known to the little colonials of America.

Newbery's literary associations, too, were both numerous and important. Before Oliver Goldsmith began to write for children, he is thought to have contributed articles for Newbery's "Literary Magazine" about seventeen hundred and fifty-eight, while Johnson's celebrated "Idler" was first printed in a weekly journal started by the publisher about the same time. For the "British Magazine" Newbery engaged Smollett as editor. In this periodical appeared Goldsmith's "History of Miss Stanton." When later this was published as "The Vicar of Wakefield," it contained a characterization of the bookseller as a good-natured man with red, pimpled face, "who was no sooner alighted than he was in haste to be gone, for he was ever on business of the utmost importance, and he was at that time actually compiling materials for the history of Mr. Thomas Trip."* With such an acquaintance it is probable that Newbery often turned to Goldsmith, Giles Jones, and Tobias Smollett for assistance in writing or abridging the various children's tales; even the pompous Dr. Johnson is said to have had a hand in their production—since he expressed a wish to do so. Newbery himself, however, assumed the responsibility as well as the credit of so many little "Histories," that it is exceedingly difficult to fix upon the real authors of some of the best-known volumes in the publisher's juvenile library.

The histories of "Goody Two-Shoes" and "Tommy Trip" (once such nursery favorites, and now almost, if not quite,

* Foster, *Life of Goldsmith*, vol. i, p. 244.

forgotten) have been attributed to various men; but according to Mr. Pearson in "Banbury Chap-Books," Goldsmith confessed to writing both. Certainly, his sly wit and quizzical vein of humor seem to pervade "Goody Two-Shoes"—often ascribed to Giles Jones—and the notes affixed to the rhymes of Mother Goose before she became Americanized. Again his skill is seen in the adaptation of "Wonders of Nature and Art" for juvenile admirers; and for "Fables in Verse" he is generally considered responsible. As all these tales were printed in the colonies or in the young Republic, their peculiarities and particularities may be better described when dealing with the issues of the American press.

John Newbery, the most illustrious of publishers in the eyes of the old-fashioned child, died in 1767, at the comparatively early age of fifty-four. Yet before his death he had proved his talent for producing at least fifty original little books, to be worth considerably more than the Biblical ten talents.

No sketch of Newbery's life should fail to mention another large factor in his successful experiment—the insertion in the "London Chronicle" and other newspapers of striking and novel advertisements of his gilt volumes, which were to be had for "six-pence the price of binding." An instance of his skill appeared in the "London Chronicle" for December 19, 1764–January 1, 1765:

"The Philosophers, Politicians, Necromancers, and the learned in every faculty are desired to observe that on the 1st of January, being New Year's Day (oh, that we may all lead new lives!) Mr. Newbery intends to publish the following important volumes, bound and gilt, and hereby invites all his little friends who are good to call for them at the Bible and Sun in St. Paul's Churchyard, but those who are naughty to have none."*

Christopher Smart, his brother-in-law, who was an adept in the art of puffing, possibly wrote many of the advertisements of new books—notices so cleverly phrased that they could not fail to attract the attention of many a country shop-keeper. In this way thousands were sold to the country districts; and book-dealers in the American commonwealths, reading the English papers and alert to improve their trade, imported them in considerable quantities.

After Newbery's death, his son, Francis, and Carnan, his stepson, carried on the business until seventeen hundred and eighty-eight; from that year until eighteen hundred and two Edward Newbery (a nephew of the senior Newbery), who in seventeen hundred and sixty-seven had set up a rival establishment, continued to publish new editions of the same little works. Yet the credit of this experiment of printing juvenile stories belongs entirely to the older publisher. Through them he made a strong protest against the reading by children of the lax chap-book literature, so excellently described by Mr. John Ashton in "Chap-Books of the Eighteenth Century;" and although his stories occasionally alluded to disagreeable subjects or situations, these were unfortunately familiar to his small patrons.

The gay little covers of gilt or parti-colored paper in which this English publisher dressed his books expressed

* Welsh, *Bookseller of the Last Century*, p. 109.

an evident purpose to afford pleasure, which was increased by the many illustrations that adorned the pages and added interest to the contents.

To the modern child, these books give no pleasure; but to those who love the history of children of the past, they are interesting for two reasons. In them is portrayed something of the life of eighteenth century children; and by them the century's difference in point of view as to the constituents of a story-book can be gauged. Moreover, all Newbery's publications are to be credited with a careful preparation that later stories sadly lacked. They were always written with a certain art; if the language was pompous, we remember Dr. Johnson; if the style was formal, its composition was correct; if the tales lacked ease in telling, it was only the starched etiquette of the day reduced to a printed page; and if they preached, they at least were seldom vulgar.

The preaching, moreover, was of different character from that of former times. Hitherto, the fear of the Lord had wholly occupied the author's attention when he composed a book "proper for a child as soon as he can read;" now, material welfare was dwelt upon, and a good boy's reward came to him when he was chosen the Lord Mayor of London. Good girls were not forgotten, and were assured that, like Goody Two-Shoes, they should attain a state of prosperity wherein

"Their Fortune and their Fame would fix
And gallop in their Coach and Six."

Goody Two-Shoes, with her particular method of instilling the alphabet, and such books as "King Pippin" (a prodigy of learning) may be considered as tiny commentaries upon the years when Johnson reigned supreme in the realm of learning. These and many others emphasized not the effects of piety,—Cotton Mather's forte,—but the benefits of learning; and hence the good boy was also one who at the age of five spelt "apple-pye" correctly and therefore eventually became a great man.

At the time of Newbery's death it was more than evident that his experiment had succeeded, and children's stories were a printed fact.

CHAPTER III

1750–1776

Kings should be good
Not men of blood.

The New England Primer, 1791

If Faith itself has different dresses worn
What wonder modes in wit should take their turn.

POPE : *Essay on Man*

CHAPTER III

1750–1776

Newbery's Books in America

IN the middle of the eighteenth century Thursdays were red-letter days for the residents of the Quaker town of Philadelphia. On that day Thomas Bradford sent forth from the "Sign of the Bible" in Second Street the weekly number of the "Pennsylvania Journal," and upon the same day his rival journalists, Franklin and Hall, issued the "Pennsylvania Gazette."

On Thursday, the fifteenth of November, seventeen hundred and fifty, Old Style, the good people of the town took up their newspapers with doubtless a feeling of comfortable anticipation, as they drew their chairs to the fireside and began to look over the local occurrences of the past week, the "freshest foreign advices," and the various bits of information that had filtered slowly from the northern and more southern provinces.

On this particular evening the subscribers to both newspapers found a trifle more news in the "Journal," but in each paper the same domestic items of interest, somewhat differently worded. The latest news from Boston was that of November fifth, from New York, November eighth, the Annapolis item was dated October tenth, and the few lines from London had been written in August.

The "Gazette" (a larger sheet than the "Journal") occasionally had upon its first page some timely article of political or local interest. But more frequently there appeared in its first column an effusion of no local color, but full of sentimental or moral reflections. In this day's issue there was a long letter, dated New York, from one who claimed to be "Beauty's Votary." This expressed the writer's disappointment that an interesting "Piece" inserted in the "Gazette" a fortnight earlier had presented in its conclusion "an unexpected shocking Image." The shock to the writer it appears was the greater, because the beginning of the article had, he thought, promised a strong contrast between "Furious Rage in our rough Sex, and Gentle mildness adorn'd with Beauty's charms in the other." The rest of the letter was an apostrophe to the fair sex in the sentimental and florid language of the period.

To the women, we imagine, this letter was more acceptable than to the men, who found the shipping news more to their taste, and noted with pleasure the arrival of the ship Carolina and the Snow Strong, which brought cargoes valuable for their various industries.

Advertisements filled a number of columns. Among them was one so novel in its character that it must have caught the eye of all readers. The middle column on the second page was devoted almost entirely to an announcement that John Newbery had for "Sale to Schoolmasters, Shopkeepers, &c, who buy in quantities to sell again," "The Museum," "A new French Primer," "The Royal Battledore," and "The Pretty Book for Children." This notice—a reduced fac-simile of which is given—made Newbery's début in Philadelphia; and it must not be forgotten that but a short period had elapsed since his first book had been printed in England.

Franklin had doubtless heard of the publisher in St. Paul's

A MUSEUM for young GENTLEMEN and LADIES:
Or, A private TUTOR for little MASTERS and MISSES.
Containing a Variety of uſeful Subjects; and in particular,

I. Directions for reading with Eloquence and Propriety.
II. The antient and preſent State of *Great Britain*; with a compendious Hiſtory of *England*.
III. An Account of the ſolar Syſtem.
IV. Hiſtorical and Geographical Deſcription of the ſeveral Countries in the World; with the Manners, Cuſtoms, and Habits of the People.
V. An Account of the Arts and Sciences.
VI. Rules for Behaviour.
VII. Advices to young Perſons on their entering upon the World; with ſhort Rules of Religion and Morality.
VIII. Tables of Weights and Meaſures.
IX. Explanation of Abbreviations uſed in Words and Dates.
X. A Deſcription of *Weſtminſter-Abbey*, St. *Paul's Church*; with the *Tower*, and *Monument* in *London*.
XI. The ſeven Wonders of the World.
XII. Proſpect and Deſcription of the burning Mountain.
XIII. Dying Words and Behaviour of great Men, when juſt quitting the Stage of Life; with many other uſeful Particulars, all in a plain familiar Way for Youth of both Sexes.

Interſperſed with LETTERS, TALES, and FABLES, for Amuſement and Inſtruction, and illustrated with CUTS.
(Being a Second Volume to the *Pretty Book for Children*.)
London, printed for J. Hodges, on the Bridge; J. Newberry, in St. Paul's Church-yard, and B. Collins, in Saliſbury.

Alſo

Lately Publiſh'd, being a very proper Book for Children, or young Perſons that are learning French, *(Price Six Pence, neatly bound, and adorn'd with Cuts,*

A New FRENCH PRIMER; Or, ALPHABET ROYAL:
ou GUIDE Commode & agréable
Dans L'ART DE LIRE,
Pour ſervir d'Introduction
Au CERCLE DES SCIENCES
Public par AUTORITE.

A Londres, pour J. Newbery, a l'enſeigne de la Bible & du Soleil, Cimetiere de S. Paul, & B. Collins, a Saliſbury. An Allowance will be made on both the above Books, to thoſe that buy them by the Dozen to ſell again.

By AUTORITY.

Lately publiſhed in London, for the Uſe of *Schools and private Families*, and humbly addreſs'd to the *Parents, Guardians, Governeſſes, School-Maſters, &c. in* Great-Britain *and* Ireland, *viz.*

The ROYAL BATTLEDORE:
OR,
FIRSTT BOOK *for* CHILDREN:

BEING the *Alphabet*, or Twenty-four Letters, Great and Small, laid down in a plain, eaſy, and entertaining Manner, in order to induce Children to learn their Letters; together with the double Letters, the firſt Syllables, Lord's Prayer, Figures, &c. Adorn'd with *Twenty-four* Cuts, and Explanations to each, adapted to the Capacities even of Children who have but juſt learn'd to ſpeak. Neatly Bound, Gilt and Glaz'd, Price *only Two-pence.*

(After which the next proper Book for Children is)

The ROYAL PRIMER:
Or, *an* EASY *and* PLEASANT GUIDE *to the* ART *of* READING.

INTERSPERSED with a great variety of pleaſant and diverting Stories, with ſuitable Morals and Reflections; which are convey'd to their tender Minds by a Number of entertaining and religious Inſtructions.

Children like tender *Oziers* take the Bow,
And as they firſt are faſhion'd always grow. DRYDEN.

Embelliſhed with *Twenty-ſeven* Cuts, and neatly Bound and Gilt. Price *only Three-pence.*

(The next Book to be learn'd after the Primer is)

The PRETTY BOOK *for* CHILDREN:
Or, An EASY GUIDE *to the* ENGLISH TONGUE,

SO well adapted to their Capacities, that it fully anſwers the End of a Child's Guide, Spelling Books, Pſalter, and Hiſtory Book. Deſign'd for the eaſy Inſtruction of thoſe that cannot read, as well as for the Entertainment of thoſe that can. And conſiſts of, 1ſt. The *Alphabet* diſpos'd in *Squares*. 2d. The *Alphabet* in different *Characters*. 3d. The *Vowels* and *Conſonants*. 4th. Eaſy *Syllables*, and Words of one, two, and three Syllables. 5th. Eaſy *Leſſons*, Scripture-Hiſtories, Fables, Stories, Moral and Religious Precepts, Proverbs, Maxims, Riddles, Verſes, Numbers, Jeſts, &c. 6th. Dialogues, Prayers, Graces, &c. The Fourth Edition, wrote in a familiar eaſy Style. Adorn'd with *Thirteen* Cuts, and neatly Bound and Gilt; and is the cheapeſt as well as the moſt uſeful Book of the Kind yet publiſhed. Price *only Six-pence.*

---------*Train up a Child in the Way he ſhould go, and when he is old he will not depart from it.* K. SOLOMON.

London: Printed and Sold by J. Newberry, in St. Paul's Church-Yard; J. Hodges on the Bridge; and B. Collins, Bookſeller, on the New Canal in Saliſbury. By whom good Allowance is made to all Shop-keepers, School-Maſters, &c. who buy Quantities to ſell again.

John Newbery's Advertisement of Children's Books

Churchyard through Mr. Strahan, his correspondent, who filled orders for him from London booksellers; but the omission of the customary announcement of special books as "to be had of the Printer hereof" points to Newbery's enterprise in seeking a wider market for his wares, and Franklin's business ability in securing the advertisement, as it is not repeated in the "Journal."

This "Museum" was probably a newer book than the "Royal Primer," "Battledore," and "Pretty Book," and consequently was more fully described; and oddly enough, all of these books are of earlier editions than Mr. Welsh, Newbery's biographer, was able to trace in England.

"The Museum" still clings to the same idea which pervaded "The Play-thing." Its second title reads: "A private TUTOR for little MASTERS and MISSES." The contents show that this purpose was carried out. It tutored them by giving directions for reading with eloquence and propriety; by presenting "the antient and present State of *Great Britain* with a compendious History of *England*;" by instructing them in "the Solar System, geography, Arts and Sciences" and the inevitable "Rules for Behaviour, Religion and Morality;" and it admonished them by giving the "Dying Words of Great Men when just quitting the Stage of Life." As a museum it included descriptions of the Seven Wonders of the World, Westminster Abbey, St. Paul's Churchyard, and the Tower of London, with an ethnological section in the geographical department! All of this amusement was to be had for the price of "One Shilling," neatly bound, with, thrown in as good measure, "Letters, Tales and Fables illustrated with Cuts."

Such a library, complete in itself, was a fine and most welcome reward for scholarship, when prizes were awarded at the end of the school session.

Importations of "Parcels of entertaining books for children" had earlier in the year been announced through the columns of the "Gazette;" but these importations, though they show familiarity with Newbery's quaint phraseology in advertising, probably also included an assortment of such little chap-books as "Tom Thumb," "Cinderella" (from the French of Monsieur Perrault), and some few other old stories which the children had long since appropriated as their own property.

In 1751 we find New York waking up to the appreciation of children's books. There J. Waddell and James Parker were apparently the pioneers in bringing to public notice the fact that they had for sale little novel-books in addition to horn-books and primers; and moreover the "Weekly Post-Boy" advertised that these booksellers had "Pretty Books for little Masters and Misses" (clearly a Newbery imitation), "with Blank Flourished Christmas pieces for Scholars."

But as yet even Franklin had hardly been convinced that the old way of imparting knowledge was not superior to the then modern combination of amusement and instruction; therefore, although with his partner, David Hall, he without doubt sold such children's books as were available, for his daughter Sally, aged seven, he had other views. At his request his wife, in December, 1751, wrote the following letter to William Strahan:

MADAM,—I am ordered by my Master to write for him Books for Sally Franklin. I am in Hopes She will be abel to write for herself by the Spring.

8 Sets of the Perceptor best Edit.
8 Doz. of Croxall's Fables.
3 Doz. of Bishop Kenns Manual for Winchester School.
1 Doz. Familiar Forms, Latin and Eng.
Ainsworth's Dictionaries, 4 best Edit.
2 Doz. Select Tales and Fables.
2 Doz. Costalio's Test.
Cole's Dictionarys Latin and Eng. 6 a half doz.
3 Doz. of Clarke's Cordery. 1 Boyle's Pliny 2 vols. 8vo.
6 Sets of Nature displayed in 7 vols. 12mo.
One good Quarto Bibel with Cudes bound in calfe.
1 Penrilla. 1 Art of making Common Salt. By Browning.

My Dafter gives her duty to Mr. Stroyhan and his Lady, and her compliments to Master Billy and all his brothers and Sisters. . . .

Your humbel Servant

DEBORAH FRANKLIN

Little Sally Franklin could not have needed eight dozen copies of Aesop's Fables, nor four Ainsworth's Dictionaries, so it is probable that Deborah Franklin's far from ready pen put down the book order for the spring, and that Sally herself was only to be supplied with the "Perceptor," the "Fables," and the "one good Quarto Bibel."

As far as it is now possible to judge, the people of the

towns soon learned the value of Newbery's little nursery tales, and after seventeen hundred and fifty-five, when most of his books were written and published, they rapidly gained a place on the family book-shelves in America.

By seventeen hundred and sixty Hugh Gaine, printer, publisher, patent medicine seller, and employment agent for New York, was importing practically all the Englishman's juvenile publications then for sale. At the "Bible and Crown," where Gaine printed the "Weekly Mercury," could be bought, wholesale and retail, such books as, "Poems for Children Three Feet High," "Tommy Trapwit," "Trip's Book of Pictures," "The New Year's Gift," "The Christmas Box," etc.

Gaine himself was a prominent printer in New York in the latter half of the eighteenth century. Until the Revolution his shop was a favorite one and well patronized. But when the hostilities began, the condition of his pocket seems to have regulated his sympathies, and he was by turn Whig and Tory according to the possession of New York by so-called Rebels, or King's Servants. When the British army evacuated New York, Gaine, wishing to keep up his trade, dropped the "Crown" from his sign. Among the enthusiastic patriots this ruse had scant success. In Freneau's political satire of the bookseller, the first verse gives a strong suggestion of the ridicule to follow:

"And first, he was, in his own representation,
A printer, once of good reputation.
He dwelt in the street called Hanover-Square,
(You 'll know where it is if you ever was there

Next door to the dwelling of Mr. Brownjohn,
Who now to the drug-shop of Pluto is gone)
But what do I say — who e'er came to town,
And knew not Hugh Gaine at the *Bible* and *Crown*."

A contemporary of, and rival bookseller to, Gaine in seventeen hundred and sixty was James Rivington. Mr. Hildeburn has given Rivington a rather unenviable reputation; still, as he occasionally printed (?) a child's book, Mr. Hildeburn's remarks are quoted:

"Until the advent of Rivington it was generally possible to tell from an American Bookseller's advertisement in the current newspapers whether the work offered for sale was printed in America or England. But the books he received in every fresh invoice from London were 'just published by James Rivington' and this form was speedily adopted by other booksellers, so that after 1761 the advertisement of books is no longer a guide to the issues of the colonial press."

Although Rivington did not set up a press until about seventeen hundred and seventy-three,—according to Mr. Hildeburn,—he had a book-shop much earlier. Here he probably reprinted the title-page and then put an elaborate notice in the "Weekly Mercury" for November 17, 1760, as follows:

JAMES RIVINGTON

Bookseller and Stationer from London over against the Golden Key in Hanover Square.

This day is published, Price, seven Shillings, and sold by the said JAMES RIVINGTON, adorned with two hundred Pictures

THE
FABLES OF AESOP

with a moral to each Fable in Verse, and an Application in Prose, intended for the Use of the youngest of readers, and proper to be put into the hands of Children, immediately after they have done with the Spelling-Book, it being adapted to their tender Capacities, the Fables are related in a short and lively Manner, and they are recommended to all those who are concerned in the education of Children. This is an entire new Work, elegantly printed and ornamented with much better Cuts than any other Edition of Aesop's Fables. Be pleased to ask for DRAPER'S AESOP.

From such records of parents' care as are given in Mrs. Charles Pinckney's letters to her husband's agent in London, and Josiah Quincy's reminiscences of his early training, it seems very evident that John Locke's advice in "Thoughts on Education" was read and followed at this time in the American colonies. Therefore, in accordance with the bachelor philosopher's theory as to reading-matter for little children, the bookseller recommended the "Fables" to "those concerned in the education of children." It is at least a happy coincidence that one of the earliest books (as far as is known to the writer), aside from school and religious books, issued as published in America for children, should have been the one Locke had so heartily recommended. This is what he had said many years previously: "When by these gentle ways he begins to *read*, some easy pleasant Book, suited to his capacities, should be put into his Hands, wherein the Entertainment that he finds might draw him on, and reward his Pains in Reading, and yet not such as will fill his head with perfectly useless Trumpery, or lay the Principles of Vice and Folly. To this

Purpose, I think Aesop's Fables the best which being Stories apt to delight and entertain a child, may yet afford useful Reflections to a grown Man.... If his Aesop has pictures in it, it will entertain him much better and encourage him to read." The two hundred pictures in Rivington's edition made it, of course, high priced in comparison with Newbery's books: but New York then contained many families well able to afford this outlay to secure such an acquisition to the family library.

Hugh Gaine at this time, as a rule, received each year two shipments of books, among which were usually some for children, yet about 1762 he began to try his own hand at reprinting Newbery's now famous little duodecimos.

In that year we find an announcement through the "New York Mercury" that he had himself printed "Divers diverting books for infants." The following list gives some idea of their character:

Just published by Hugh Gaine

A pretty Book for Children; Or an Easy Guide to the English Tongue.

The private Tutor for little Masters and Misses.

Food for the Mind; or a new Riddle Book compiled for the use of little Good Boys and Girls in America. By Jack the Giant-Killer, Esq.

A Collection of Pretty Poems, by Tommy Tag, Esq.

Aesop's Fables in Verse, with the Conversation of Beasts and Birds, at their several Meetings. By Woglog the great Giant.

A Little pretty Book, intended for the Amusement of Little Master Tommy and pretty Miss Polly, with two Letters from Jack the Giant-Killer.

Be Merry and Wise: Or the Cream of the Jests. By Tommy Trapwit, Esq.

The title of "Food for the Mind" is of special importance, since in it Gaine made a clever alteration by inserting the words "Good Boys and Girls in *America*." The colonials were already beginning to feel a pride in the fact of belonging to the new country, America, and therefore Gaine shrewdly changed the English title to one more likely to induce people to purchase.

Gaine and Rivington alone have left records of printing children's story-books in the town of New York before the Revolution; but before they began to print, other booksellers advertised their invoices of books. In 1759 Garrat Noel, a Dutchman, had announced that he had "the very prettiest gilt Books for little Masters and Misses that ever were invented, full of wit and wisdom, at the surprising low Price of only one Shilling each finely bound and adorned with a number of curious Cuts." By 1762 Noel had increased his stock and placed a somewhat larger advertisement in the "Mercury" of December 27. The late arrival of his goods may have been responsible for the bargains he offered at this holiday sale.

GARRAT NOEL *Begs Leave to Inform the Public, that according to his Annual Custom, he has provided a very large Assortment of Books for Entertainment and Improvement of Youth, in Reading, Writing, Cyphering, and Drawing, as Proper Presents at* CHRISTMAS *and* New-Year.

The following Small, but improving Histories, are sold at *Two Shillings*, each, neatly bound in red, and adorn'd with Cuts.

☞Those who buy *Six*, shall have a *Seventh Gratis*, and buying only *Three*, they shall have a present of a fine large Copper-Plate Christmas Piece: [*List of histories follows.*]

The following neat Gilt Books, very instructive and Amusing being full of Pictures, are sold at *Eighteen Pence* each.

> Fables in Verse and Prose, with the Conversation of Birds & Beasts at their several meetings, Routs and Assemblies for the Improvement of Old and Young, etc.

To-day none of these gay little volumes sold in New York are to be seen. The inherent faculty of children for losing and destroying books, coupled with the perishable nature of these toy volumes, has rendered the children's treasures of seventeen hundred and sixty-two a great rarity. The Historical Society of Pennsylvania is the fortunate possessor of one much prized story-book printed in that year; but though it is at present in the Quaker City, a printer of Boston was responsible for its production.

In Isaiah Thomas's recollections of the early Boston printers, he described Zechariah Fowle, with whom he served his apprenticeship, and Samuel Draper, Fowle's partner. These men, about seventeen hundred and fifty-seven, took a house in Marlborough Street. Here, according to Thomas, "they printed and opened a shop. They kept a great supply of ballads, and small pamphlets for book pedlars, of whom there were many at that time. Fowle was bred to the business, but he was an indifferent hand at the press, and much worse at the case."

This description of the printer's ability is borne out by the "New-Gift for Children," printed by this firm. It is probably the oldest story-book bearing an American imprint now in existence, and for this reason merits description, although its contents can be seen in the picture of the title-page. Brown with age and like all chap-books without a cover — for it was Newbery who introduced this more durable and attractive feature — all sizes in type were used to print its fifteen stories. The stories in themselves were not new, as it is called the "Fourth edition." It is possible that they were taken from the Banbury chap-books, which also often copied Newbery's juvenile library, as the list of his publications compiled by Mr. Charles Welsh does not contain this title.

The loyalty of the Boston printers found expression on the third page by a very black cut of King George the Third, who appears rather puzzled and not a little unhappy; but it found favor with customers, for as yet the colonials thought their king "no man of blood." On turning the page Queen Charlotte looks out with goggle-eyes, curls, and a row of beads about the size of pebbles around her thick neck. The picture seems to be a copy from some miniature of the queen, as an oval frame with a crown surmounting it encircles the portrait. The stories are so much better than some that were written even after the nineteenth century, that extracts from them are worth reading. The third tale, called "The Generosity of Confessing a Fault," begins as follows:

"Miss *Fanny Goodwill* was one of the prettiest children that ever was seen; her temper was as sweet as her looks, and her behavior so genteel and obliging that everybody admir'd her; for nobody can help loving good children, any more than they can help being angry with those that are naughty. It is

A

New Gift for Children.

Containing

Delightful and Entertaining

STORIES

In TWO PARTS;

VIZ.

1. The Dutiful Child.
2. The Thief.
3. The Generosity of confessing a Fault.
4. The two good Friends.
5. The Rewards of Virtue.

SECOND PART.

6. The Good Boy.
7. The Good Girl.
8. The Proud Play-mate.
9. The good Girl and the pretty Girl.
10. The meanly proud Girl.
11. The Trifler.
12. The undutiful Child.
13. The lost Child.
14. The Advantages of Truth.
15. Of Tommy Fido.

The FOURTH EDITION.

Adorn'd with *CUTS*.

Boston; New-England: Printed and Sold by *Fowle* & *Draper*, in Marlboro'-Street.
M,DCC,LXII.

Title-page from "The New Gift for Children"

no wonder then that her papa and mama lov'd her dearly, they took a great deal of pains to improve her mind so that before she was seven years old, she could read, and talk, and work like a little woman. One day as her papa was sitting by the fire, he set her upon his knees, kiss'd her, and told her how very much he lov'd her; and then smiling, and taking hold of her hand, My dear Fanny, said he, take care never to tell a lye, and then I shall always love you as well as I do now. You or I may be guilty of a fault; but there is something noble and generous in owning our errors, and striving to mend them; but a lye more than doubles the fault, and when it is found out, makes the lyar appear mean and contemptible. . . . Thus, my dear, the lyar is a wretch, whom nobody trusts, nobody regards, nobody pities. Indeed papa, said Miss *Fanny*, I would not be such a creature for all the world. You are very good, my little *charmer*, said her papa and kiss'd her again."

The inevitable temptation came when Miss Fanny went on "a visit to a Miss in the neighborhood; her mama ordered her to be home at eight o'clock; but she was engag'd at play, and did not mind how the time pass'd, so that she stay'd till near ten; and then her mama sent for her." The child of course was frightened by the lateness of the hour, and the maid—who appears in the illustration with cocked hat and musket!—tried to calm her fears with the advice to "tell her mama that the Miss she went to see had taken her out." "*No Mary*, said Miss *Fanny*, wiping her pretty eyes, I am above a lye;" and she rehearsed for the benefit of the maid her father's admonition.

Story IX tells of the *Good Girl and Pretty Girl.* In this the pretty child had bright eyes and pretty plump cheeks and was much admired. She, however, was a meanly proud girl, and so naughty as not to want to grow wiser, but applied to those good people who happened to be less favored in looks such terms as "bandy-legs, crump, and all such naughty names." The good sister "could read before the pretty miss could tell a letter; and though her shape was not so genteel her behavior was a great deal more so. But alas! the pretty creature fell sick of the small-pox, and all her beauty vanished." Thus in the eighteenth century was the adage "Beauty is but skin deep" brought to bear upon conduct.

On the last page is a cut of "Louisburg demolished," which had served its time already upon almanacs, but the eight cuts were undoubtedly made especially for children. Moreover, since they do not altogether illustrate the various stories, they are good proof that similar chap-book tales were printed by Fowle and Draper for little ones before the War of Independence.

In the southern provinces the sea afforded better transportation facilities for household necessities and luxuries than the few post-lines from the north could offer. Bills of exchange could be drawn against London, to be paid by the profits of the tobacco crops, a safer method of payment than any that then existed between the northern and southern towns. In the regular orders sent by George Washington to Robert Carey in London, twice we find mention of the children's needs and wishes. In the very first invoice of goods to be shipped to Washington after his marriage with Mrs. Custis in seventeen hundred and fifty-nine, he ordered "10 Shillings worth of Toys, 6 little books for children beginning to read and a fashionable dressed baby to cost 10 Shillings;" and again later in ordering clothes, "Toys, Sugar, Images and Comfits" for his step-children he added: "Books according to the enclosed list to be charged equally to John Parke Custis and Martha Parke Custis."

But in Boston the people bought directly from the booksellers, of whom there were already many. One of these was John Mein, who played a part in the historic Non-Importation Agreement. In seventeen hundred and fifty this Englishman had opened in King Street a shop which he called the "London Book-Store." Here he sold many imported books, and in seventeen hundred and sixty-five, when the population of Boston numbered some twenty thousand, he started the "earliest circulating library, advertised to contain ten thousand volumes."* This shop was both famous and notorious: famous because of its "Very Grand Assortment of the most modern Books;" notorious because of the accusations made against its owner when the colonials, aroused by the action of Parliament, passed the Non-Importation Agreement.

Before the excitement had culminated in this "Agreement," John Mein's lists of importations show that the children's pleasure had not been forgotten, and after it their books singularly enough were connected with this historic action.

In 1766, in the "Boston Evening Post," we find Mein's announcement that "Little Books with Pictures for Children" could be purchased at the London Book-Store; in December,

* Winsor, *Memorial History of Boston*, vol. ii, p. xix.

1767, he advertised through the columns of the "Boston Chronicle," among other books, "in every branch of polite literature," a "Great Variety of entertaining Books for Children, proper for presents at Christmas or New-year's day — Prices from Two Coppers to Two Shillings." In August of the following year Mein gave the names of seven of Newbery's famous gilt volumes, as "to be sold" at his shop. These "pretty little entertaining and instructive Books" were "Giles Gingerbread," the "Adventures of little Tommy Trip with his dog Jouler," "Tommy Trip's Select Fables," and "an excellent Pastoral Hymn," "The Famous Tommy Thumb's Little Story-Book," "Leo, the Great Giant," and "Urax, or the Fair Wanderer — price eight pence lawful money. *A very interesting tale in which the protection of the Almighty* is proved to be the first and chief support of the Female Sex." Number seven in the list was the story of the "Cruel Giant Barbarico," and it is one of this edition that is now among the rare Americana of the Boston Public Library. The imprint upon its title-page coincides with Isaiah Thomas's statement that though "Fleming was not concerned with Mein in bookselling, several books were printed at their house for Mein." Its date, 1768, would indicate that Mein had reproduced one of his importations to which allusion has already been made. The book in marbled covers, time-worn and faded now, was sold for only "six-pence lawful" when new, possibly because it lacked illustrations.

One year later, when the Non-Importation Agreement had passed and was rigorously enforced in the port of Boston, these same little books were advertised again in the "Chroni-

Miss Fanny's Maid

cle" of December 4–7 under the large caption, PRINTED IN AMERICA AND TO BE SOLD BY JOHN MEIN. Times had so changed within one year's space that even a child's six-penny book was unpopular, if known to have been imported.

Mein was among those accused of violating the "Agreement;" he was charged with the importation of materials for book-making. In a November number of the "Chronicle" of seventeen hundred and sixty-nine, Mein published an article entitled "A State of the Importation from Great Britain into the Port of BOSTON with the advertisement of a set of Men, who assume to themselves THE TITLE of *ALL the Well Disposed Merchants*." In this letter the London Book-Store proprietor vigorously defended himself, and protested that the quantity of his work necessitated some importations not procurable in Boston. He also made sarcastic references to other men whom he thought the cap fitted better with less excuse. It was in the following December that he tried to keep this trade in children's books by his apparently patriotic announcement regarding them. His protests were useless. Already in disfavor with some because he was supposed to print books in America but used a London imprint, his popularity waned; he was marked as a loyalist, and there was little of the spirit of tolerance for such in that hot-bed of patriotism. The air was so full of the growing differences between the colonials and the king's government, that in seventeen hundred and seventy Mein closed out his stock and returned to England.

On the other hand, the patriotic booksellers did not fail to take note of the crystallization of public opinion. Robert Bell in Philadelphia appended a note to his catalogue of books, stating that "The Lovers and Practisers of Patriotism are requested to note that all the Books in this Catalogue are either of American manufacture, or imported before the Non-Importation Agreement."

The supply of home-made paper was of course limited. So much was needed to circulate among the colonies pamphlets dealing with the injustice of the king's government toward his American subjects, that it seems remarkable that any juvenile books should have been printed in those stirring days before the war began. It is rather to be expected that, with the serious turn that events had taken and the consequent questions that had arisen, the publications of the American press should have received the shadow of the forthcoming trouble — a shadow sufficient to discourage any attempt at humor for adult or child. Evidence, however, points to the fact that humor and amusement were not totally lacking in the issues of the press of at least one printer in Boston, John Boyle. The humorous satire produced by his press in seventeen hundred and seventy-five, called "The First Book of the American Chronicles of the Times," purported to set forth the state of political affairs during the troubles "wherein all our calamities are seen to flow from the fact that the king had set up for our worship the god of the heathen — The Tea Chest." This pamphlet has been one to keep the name of John Boyle among the prominent printers of pre-Revolutionary days. Additional interest accrues for this reason to a play-book printed by Boyle—the only one extant of this decade known to the writer.

This quaint little chap-book, three by four inches in size, was issued in seventeen hundred and seventy-one, soon after Boyle had set up his printing establishment and four years before the publication of the famous pamphlet. It represents fully the standard for children's literature in the days when Newbery's tiny classics were making their way to America, and was indeed advertised by Mein in seventeen hundred and sixty-eight among the list of books "Printed in America." Its title, "The Famous Tommy Thumb's Little Story-Book: Containing his Life and Adventures," has rather a familiar sound, but its contents would not now be allowed upon any nursery table. Since the days of the Anglo-Saxons, Tom Thumb's adventures have been told and retold; each generation has given to the rising generation the version thought proper for the ears of children. In Boyle's edition this method resulted in realism pushed to the extreme; but it is not to be denied that the yellowed pages contain the wondrous adventures and hairbreadth escapes so dear to the small boy of all time. The thrilling incidents were further enlivened, moreover, by cuts called by the printer "*curious*" in the sense of very fine: and *curious* they are to-day because of the crudeness of their execution and the coarseness of their design. Nevertheless, the grotesque character of the illustrations was altogether effective in impressing upon the reader the doughty deeds of his old friend, Tom Thumb. The book itself shows marks of its popularity, and of the hard usage to which it was subjected by its happy owner, who was not critical of the editor's freedom of speech.

The coarseness permitted in a nursery favorite makes it

sufficiently clear that the standard for the ideal toy-book of the eighteenth century is no gauge for that of the twentieth. Child-life differed in many particulars, as Mr. Julian Hawthorne pointed out some years ago, when he wrote that the children of the eighteenth century "were urged to grow up almost before they were short-coated." We must bear this in mind in turning to another class of books popular with adult and child alike in both England and America before and for some years after the Revolution.

This was the period when the novel in the hands of Richardson, Fielding, and Smollett was assuming hitherto unsuspected possibilities. Allusion must be made to some of the characteristics of their work, since their style undoubtedly affected juvenile reading and the tales written for children.

Taking for the sake of convenience the novels of the earliest of this group of men, Samuel Richardson, as a starting-point, we find in Pamela and Mr. Lovelace types of character that merge from the Puritanical concrete examples of virtue and vice into a psychological attempt to depict the emotion and feeling preceding every act of heroine and villain. Through every stage of the story the author still clings to the long-established precedent of giving moral and religious instruction. Afterwards, when Fielding attempted to parody "Pamela," he developed the novel of adventure in high and low life, and produced "Joseph Andrews." He then followed this with the character-study represented by "Tom Jones, Foundling." Richardson in "Pamela" had aimed to emphasize virtue as in the end prospering; Fielding's characters rather embody the principle of virtue being its own reward and of vice bringing its own punishment. Smollett in "Humphrey Clinker's Adventures" brought forth fun from English surroundings instead of seeking for the hero thrilling and daring deeds in foreign countries. He also added to the list of character-studies "Roderick Random," a tale of the sea, the mystery of which has never palled since "Robinson Crusoe" saw light.

There was also the novel of letters. In the age of the first great novelists letter-writing was among the polite arts. It was therefore counted a great but natural achievement when the epistolary method of revealing the plot was introduced. "Clarissa Harlowe" and "Sir Charles Grandison" were the results of this style of writing; they comprehended the "most Important Concerns of private life"—"concerns" which moved with lingering and emotional persistency towards the inevitable catastrophe in "Clarissa," and the happy issue out of the misunderstandings and misadventures which resulted in Miss Byron's alliance with Sir Charles.

Until after the next (nineteenth) century had passed its first decade these tales were read in full or abridged forms by many children among the fashionable and literary sets in England and America. Indeed, the art of writing for children was so unknown that often attempts to produce child-like "histories" for them resulted in little other than novels upon an abridged scale.

But before even abridged novels found their way into juvenile favor, it was "customary in Richardson's time to read his novels aloud in the family circle. When some pathetic passage was reached the members of the family would retire to separate apartments to weep; and after composing themselves, they would return to the fireside to have the reading proceed. It was reported to Richardson, that, on one of these occasions, 'an amiable little boy sobbed as if his sides would burst and resolved to mind his books that he might be able to read Pamela through without stopping.' That there might be something in the family novel expressly for children, Richardson sometimes stepped aside from the main narrative to tell them a moral tale." *

Mr. Cross gives an example of this which, shorn of its decoration, was the tale of two little boys and two little girls, who never told fibs, who were never rude and noisy, mischievous or quarrelsome; who always said their prayers when going to bed, and therefore became fine ladies and gentlemen.

To make the tales less difficult for amiable children to read, an abridgment of their contents was undertaken; and Goldsmith is said to have done much of the "cutting" in "Pamela," "Clarissa Harlowe," "Sir Charles Grandison," and others. These books were included in the lists of those sent to America for juvenile reading. In Boston, Cox and Berry inserted in the "Boston Gazette and Country Journal" a notice that they had the "following little Books for all good Boys and Girls:

The Brother's Gift, or the Naughty Girl Reformed.
The Sister's Gift, or the Naughty Boy Reformed.
The Hobby Horse, or Christmas Companion.
The Cries of London as Exhibited in the Streets.
The Puzzling Cap.
The History of Tom Jones.

* Cross, *Development of the English Novel*, pp. 38, 39.

The History of Joseph Andrews.	Abridg'd from the works of H. Fielding
The History of Pamela.	abridg'd from the works of Samuel Richardson, Esq.
The History of Grandison.	
The History of Clarissa."	

Up to this time the story has been rather of the books read by the Puritan and Quaker population of the colonies. There had arisen during the first half of the eighteenth century, however, a merchant class which owed its prosperity to its own ability. Such men sought for their families the material results of wealth which only a place like Boston could bestow. Many children, therefore, were sent to this town to acquire suitable education in books, accomplishments, and deportment. A highly interesting record of a child of well-to-do parents has been left by Anna Green Winslow, who came to Boston to stay with an aunt for the winters of 1771 and 1772. Her diary gives delightful glimpses of children's tea-parties, fashions, and schools, all put down with a childish disregard of importance or connection. It is in these jottings of daily occurrences that proof is found that so young a girl read, quite as a matter of course, the abridged works of Fielding and Richardson.

On January 1, 1772, she wrote in her diary, "a Happy New Year, I have bestowed no new year's gifts, as yet. But have received one very handsome one, Viz, the History of Joseph Andrews abreviated. In nice Guilt and Flowers covers." Again, she put down an account of a day's work, which she called "a piecemeal for in the first place I sew'd on the bosom of unkle's shirt, and mended two pairs of gloves, mended for the wash two handkerch'fs, (one cambrick) sewed on half a border of a lawn apron of aunt's, read part of the xxist chapter of Exodous, & a story in the Mother's Gift." Later she jotted in her book the loan of "3 of Cousin Charles' books to read, viz.—The puzzling Cap, the female Orators & the history of Gaffer Two Shoes." Little Miss Winslow, though only eleven years of age, was a typical child of the educated class in Boston, and, according to her journal, also followed the English custom of reading aloud "with Miss Winslow, the Generous Inconstant and Sir Charles Grandison." It is to be regretted that her diary gives no information as to how she liked such tales. We must anticipate some years to find a comment in the Commonplace Book of a Connecticut girl. Lucy Sheldon lived in Litchfield, a thriving town in eighteen hundred, and did much reading for a child in those days. Upon "Sir Charles Grandison" she confided to her book this offhand note: "Read in little Grandison, which shows that, virtue always meets its reward and vice is punished." The item is very suggestive of Goldsmith's success in producing an abridgment that left the moral where it could not be overlooked.

To discuss in detail this class of writings is not necessary, but a glance at the story of "Clarissa" gives an instructive impression of what old-fashioned children found zestful.

"Clarissa Harlowe" in its abridged form was first published by Newbery, Senior. The book that lies before the writer was printed in seventeen hundred and seventy-two by his son, Francis Newbery. In size five by three and one-half inches, it is decked in once gay parti-colored heavy Dutch paper, with a delicate gold tracery over all. This paper binding, called by Anna Winslow "Flowery Guilt," can no longer be found in Holland, the place of its manufacture; with sarsinet and other fascinating materials it has vanished so completely that it exists only on the faded bindings of such small books as "Clarissa."

The narrative itself is compressed from the original seven volumes into one volume of one hundred and seventy-six closely printed pages, with several full-page copper-plate illustrations. The plot, however, gains rather than loses in this condensed form. The principal distressing situations follow so fast one upon the other that the intensity of the various episodes in the *affecting* history is increased by the total absence of all the "moving" letters found in the original work. The "lordly husband and father," "the imperious son," "the proud ambitious sister, Arabella," all combined to force the universally beloved and unassuming Clarissa to marry the wealthy Mr. Somers, who was to be the means of "the aggrandisement of the family." Clarissa, in this perplexing situation, yielded in a desperate mood to "the earnest entreaties of the artful Lovelace to accept the protection of the Ladies of his family." Who these ladies were, to whom the designing Lovelace conducted the agitated heroine, is set forth in unmistakable language; and thereafter follow the treacherous behaviour exhibited by Lovelace, the various attempts to escape by the unhappy beauty, and her final exhaustion and death. An example of the style may be given in this description of the death-scene:

"Clarissa had before remarked that all would be most conveniently over in bed: The solemn, the most important moment approached, but her soul ardently aspiring after immorality [immortality was of course the author's intention], she imagined the time moved slowly; and with great presence of mind, she gave orders in relation to her body, directing her nurse and the maid of the house, as soon as she was cold, to put her into her coffin. The Colonel [her cousin], after paying her another visit, wrote to her uncle, Mr. John Harlowe, that they might save themselves the trouble of having any further debates about reconciliation; for before they could resolve, his dear cousin would probably be no more. . . .

"A day or two after, Mr. Belford [a friend] was sent for, and immediately came; at his entrance he saw the Colonel kneeling by her bed-side with the ladies right hand in both his, which his face covered bathing it with tears, though she had just been endeavoring to comfort him, in noble and elevated strains. On the opposite side of the bed was seated Mrs. Lovick, who leaning against the bed's-head in a most disconsolate manner, turned to him as soon as she saw him, crying, O Mr. Belford, the dear lady! a heavy sigh not permitting her to say more. Mrs. Smith [the landlady] was kneeling at the bed's feet with clasped fingers and uplifted eyes, with tears trickling in large drops from her cheeks, as if imploring help from the source of all comfort.

"The excellent lady had been silent a few minutes, and was thought speechless, she moving her lips without uttering a word; but when Mrs. Lovick, on Mr. Belford's approach, pronounced his name, O Mr. Belford! cried she, in a faint inward voice, Now! — now! — I bless God, all will soon be over — a few minutes will end this strife — and I shall be happy," etc. Her speech was long, although broken by dashes, and again she resumed, "in a more faint and broken accent," the blessing and directions. "She then sunk her head upon the pillow; and fainting away, drew from them her hands." Once more she returned to consciousness, "when waving her hand to him [Mr. Belford] and to her cousin, and bowing her head to every one present, not omitting the nurse and maid servant, with a faltering and inward voice, she added Bless — Bless — you all! — "

The illustrations, in comparison with others of the time, are very well engraved, although the choice of subjects is somewhat singular. The last one represents Clarissa's friend, "Miss Howe" (the loyal friend to whom all the absent letters were addressed), "lamenting over the corpse of Clarissa," who lies in the coffin ordered by the heroine "to be covered with fine black cloth, and lined with white satin."

As one lays aside this faded duodecimo, the conviction is strong that the texture of the life of an old-fashioned child was of coarser weave than is pleasant to contemplate. How else could elders and guardians have placed without scruple such books in the hands of children? The one explanation is to be found in such diaries as that of Anna Winslow, who quaintly put down in her book facts and occurrences denoting the maturity already reached by a little miss of eleven.

CHAPTER IV

1776–1790

The British King
Lost States thirteen.

The New England Primer,
Philadelphia, 1797

The good little boy
That will not tell a lie,
Shall have a plum-pudding
Or hot apple-pye.

Jacky Dandy's Delight,
Worcester, 1786

CHAPTER IV

1776–1790

Patriotic Printers and the American Newbery

WHEN John Mein was forced to close his London Book-Store in Boston and to return to England in 1770, the children of that vicinity had need to cherish their six-penny books with increased care. The shadow of impending conflict was already deep upon the country when Mein departed; and the events of the decade following seventeen hundred and seventy-three—the year of the Boston Tea-Party—were too absorbing and distressing for such trifling publications as toy-books to be more than occasionally printed. Indeed, the history of the American Revolution is so interwoven with tales of privation of the necessities of life that it is astonishing that any printer was able to find ink or paper to produce even the nursery classic "Goody Two-Shoes," printed by Robert Bell of Philadelphia in seventeen hundred and seventy-six.

In New York the conditions were different. The Loyalists, as long as the town was held by the British, continued to receive importations of goods of all descriptions. Among the booksellers, Valentine Nutter from time to time advertised children's as well as adults' books. Hugh Gaine apparently continued to reprint Newbery's duodecimos; and, in a rather newer shop, Roger and Berry's, in Hanover Square, near Gaine's, could be had "Gilt Books, together with Stationary, Jewelry, a Collection of the most books, bibles, prayer-books and patent medicines warranted genuine."

Elsewhere in the colonies, as in Boston, the children went without new books, although very occasionally such notices as the following were inserted in the newspapers:

Just imported and to be Sold by Thomas Bradford

At his Book-Store in Market-Street, adjoining the Coffee-house

The following Books . . .

Little Histories for Children,

Among which are, Book of Knowledge, Joe Miller's Jests, Jenny Twitchells' ditto, the Linnet, The Lark (being collections of best Songs), Robin Redbreast, Choice Spirits, Argalus & Parthenia, Valentine and Orson, Seven Wise Masters, Seven Wise Mistresses, Russell's seven Sermons, Death of Abel, French Convert, Art's Treasury, Complete Letter-Writer, Winter Evening Entertainment, Stories and Tales, Triumphs of Love, being a Collection of Short Stories, Joseph Andrews, Aesop's Fables, Scotch Rogue, Moll Flanders, Lives of Highwaymen, Lives of Pirates, Buccaneers of America, Robinson Crusoe, Twelve Caesars.

Such was the assortment of penny-dreadfuls and religious tracts offered in seventeen hundred and eighty-one to the Philadelphia public for juvenile reading. It is typical of the chapmen's library peddled about the colonies long after they had become states. "Valentine and Orson," "The Seven Wise Masters," "The Seven Wise Mistresses," and "Winter Evening Entertainment" are found in publishers' lists for many years, and, in spite of frequent vulgarities, there was often no discrimination between them and Newbery's far superior stories; but by eighteen hundred and thirty almost all of these undesirable reprints had disappeared, being buried under the quantities of Sunday-school tales held in high favor at that date.

Meanwhile, the six years of struggle for liberty had rendered the necessaries of life in many cases luxuries. As early as seventeen hundred and seventy-five, during the siege of Boston, provisions and articles of dress had reached such prices that we find thrifty Mrs. John Adams, in Braintree, Massachusetts, foreseeing a worse condition, writing her husband, who was one of the Council assembled in Philadelphia, to send her, if possible, six thousand pins, even if they should cost five pounds. Prices continued to rise and currency to depreciate. In seventeen hundred and seventy-nine Mrs. Adams reported in her letters to her husband that potatoes were ten dollars a bushel, and writing-paper brought the same price per pound.

Yet family life went on in spite of these increasing difficulties. The diaries and letters of such remarkable women as the patriotic Abigail Adams, the Quakeress, Mrs. Eliza Drinker, the letters of the Loyalist and exile, James Murray, the correspondence of Eliza Pinckney of Charleston, and the reminiscences of a Whig family who were obliged to leave New York upon the occupation of the town by British forces, abound in those details of domestic life that give a many sided picture. Joys derived from good news of dear ones, and family reunions; anxieties occasioned by illness, or the armies' depredations; courageous efforts on the part of mothers not to allow their children's education and occupations to suffer unnecessarily; tragedies of death and ruined homes—all are recorded with a "particularity" for which we are now grateful to the writers.

It is through these writings, also, that we are allowed

glimpses of the enthusiasm for the cause of Liberty, or King, which was imbibed from the parents by the smallest children. On the Whig side, patriotic mothers in New England filled their sons with zeal for the cause of freedom and with hatred of the tyranny of the Crown; while in the more southern colonies the partisanship of the little ones was no less intense. "From the constant topic of the present conversation," wrote the Rev. John J. Zubly (a Swiss clergyman settled in South Carolina and Georgia), in an address to the Earl of Dartmouth in seventeen hundred and seventy-five, — "from the constant topic of the present conversation, every child unborn will be impressed with the notion—it is slavery to be bound at the will of another 'in all things whatsoever.' Every mother's milk will convey a detestation of this maxim. Were your lordship in America, you might see little ones acquainted with the word of command before they can distinctly speak, and shouldering of a gun before they are well able to walk."*

The children of the Tories had also their part in the struggle. To some the property of parents was made over, to save it from confiscation in the event of the success of the American cause. To others came the bitterness of separation from parents, when they were sent across the sea to unknown relatives; while again some faint manuscript record tells of a motherless child brought from a comfortable home, no longer tenable, to whatever quarters could be found within the British lines. Fortunately, children usually adapt themselves easily to changed conditions, and in the novelty and excitement of the life around them, it is probable they soon forgot the luxuries of

* Tyler, *Literary History of the American Revolution*, vol. i, p. 485.

dolls and hobby-horses, toy-books and drums, of former days.

In the Commonwealth of Pennsylvania the sentiment of the period was expressed in two or three editions of "The New England Primer." Already in 1770 one had appeared containing as frontispiece a poor wood-cut of John Hancock. In 1775 the enthusiasm over the appointment of George Washington as commander-in-chief brought out another edition of the A B C book with the same picture labelled "General Washington." The custom of making one cut do duty in several representations was so well understood that this method of introducing George Washington to the infant reader naturally escaped remark.

Another primer appeared four years later, which was advertised by Walters and Norman in the "Pennsylvania Evening Post" as "adorned with a beautiful head of George Washington and other copper-plates." According to Mr. Hildeburn, this small book had the honor of containing the first portrait of Washington engraved in America. While such facts are of trifling importance, they are, nevertheless, indications of the state of intense feeling that existed at the time, and point the way by which the children's books became nationalized.

In New England the very games of children centred in the events which thrilled the country. Josiah Quincy remembered very well in after life, how "at the age of five or six, astride my grandfather's cane and with my little whip, I performed prodigies of valor, and more than once came to my mother's knees declaring that I had driven the British out of Boston." Afterwards at Phillips Academy, in Andover, between seventeen hundred and seventy-eight and seventeen hundred and eighty-six, Josiah and his schoolfellows "established it as a principle that every hoop, sled, etc., should in some way bear *Thirteen* marks as evidence of the political character of the owner,—if which were wanting the articles became fair prize and were condemned and forfeited without judge, jury, or decree of admiralty."*

Other boys, such as John Quincy Adams, had tutors at home as a less expensive means of education than the war-time price of forty dollars a week for each child that good boarding-schools demanded. But at their homes the children had plenty of opportunity to show their intense enthusiasm for the cause of liberty. Years later, Mr. Adams wrote to a Quaker friend:

"For the space of twelve months my mother with her infant children dwelt, liable every hour of the day and of the night to be butchered in cold blood, or taken and carried to Boston as hostages. My mother lived in uninterrupted danger of being consumed with them all in a conflagration kindled by a torch in the same hands which on the Seventeenth of June [1775] lighted the fires of Charlestown."†

He was, of course, only one of many boys who saw from some height near their homes the signs of battle, the fires of the enemy's camps, the smoke rising from some farm fired by the British, or burned by its owner to prevent their occupation of it. With hearts made to beat quickly by the news that filtered through the lines, and heads made old by the responsibility thrust upon them,—in the absence of fathers and older

* *Life of Josiah Quincy*, p. 27. Boston, 1866.

† Earle, *Child Life in Colonial Days*, p. 171.

brothers,—such boys as John Quincy Adams saw active service in the capacity of post-riders bearing in their several districts the anxiously awaited tidings from Congress or battlefield.

Fortunate indeed were the families whose homes were not disturbed by the military operations. From Boston, New York, and Philadelphia, families were sent hastily to the country until the progress of the war made it possible to return to such comforts as had not been destroyed by the British soldiers. The "Memoirs of Eliza Morton," afterward Mrs. Josiah Quincy, but a child eight years of age in seventeen hundred and seventy-six, gives a realistic account of the life of such Whig refugees. Upon the occupation of New York by the British, her father, a merchant of wealth, as riches were then reckoned, was obliged to burn his warehouse to save it from English hands. Mr. Morton then gathered together in the little country village of Basking Ridge, seven miles from Morristown, New Jersey, such of his possessions as could be hastily transported from the city. Among the books saved in this way were the works of Thurston, Thomson, Lyttleton, and Goldsmith, and for the children's benefit, "Dodsley's Collection of Poems," and "Pilgrim's Progress." "This," wrote Mrs. Quincy, "was a great favorite; Mr. Greatheart was in my opinion a hero, well able to help us all on our way." During the exile from New York, as Eliza Morton grew up, she read all these books, and years afterward told her grandchildren that while she admired the works of Thurston, Thomson, and Lyttleton, "those of Goldsmith were my chief delight. When my reading became afterward more extensive I instinctively disliked the extravagant fiction which often injures the youthful mind."

The war, however, was not allowed to interfere with the children's education in this family. In company with other little exiles, they were taught by a venerable old man until the evacuation of Philadelphia made it possible to send the older children to Germantown, where a Mr. Leslie had what was considered a fine school. The schoolroom walls were hung with lists of texts of Scripture beginning with the same letter, and for globes were substituted the schoolmaster's snuff-box and balls of yarn. If these failed to impress a child with the correct notions concerning the solar system, the children themselves were made to whirl around the teacher.

In Basking Ridge the children had much excitement with the passing of soldiers to Washington's headquarters in Morristown, and with watching for "The Post" who carried the news between Philadelphia, Princeton, and Morristown. "'The Post,' Mr. Martin," wrote Mrs. Quincy, "was an old man who carried the mail, . . . he was our constant medium of communication; and always stopped at our house to refresh himself and horse, tell the news, and bring packets. He used to wear a blue coat with yellow buttons, a scarlet waistcoat, leathern small-clothes, blue yarn stockings, and a red wig and cocked hat, which gave him a sort of military appearance. He usually traveled in a sulky, but sometimes in a chaise, or on horseback. . . . Mr. Martin also contrived to employ himself in knitting coarse yarn stockings while driving or rather jogging along the road, or when seated on his saddle-bags on horseback. He certainly did not ride *post*, according to the present [1821] meaning of that term."

Deprived like many other children of Newbery's peaceful biographies and stories, the little Mortons' lives were too full of an intense daily interest to feel the lack of new literature of this sort. Tales of the campaigns told in letters to friends and neighbors were reëchoed in the ballads and songs that formed part of the literary warfare waged by Whig or Loyal partisans. Children of to-day sing so zestfully the popular tunes of the moment, that it requires very little imagination to picture the schoolboy of Revolutionary days shouting lustily verses from "The Battle of the Kegs," and other rhymed stories of military incidents. Such a ballad was "A Song for the Red Coats," written after the successful campaign against Burgoyne, and beginning:

"Come unto me, ye heroes,
Whose hearts are true and bold,
Who value more your honor,
Than others do their gold!
Give ear unto my story,
And I the truth will tell,
Concerning many a soldier,
Who for his country fell."

Children, it has been said, are good haters. To the patriot boy and girl, the opportunity to execrate Benedict Arnold was found in these lines of a patriotic "ditty" concerning the fate of Major André:

"When he was executed
He looked both meek and mild;
He looked upon the people,
And pleasantly he smiled.
It moved each eye to pity,
Caused every heart to bleed;

And every one wished him released—
And *Arnold* in his stead."[*]

Loyalist children had an almost equal supply of satirical verse to fling back at neighbors' families, where in country districts some farms were still occupied by sympathizers with Great Britain. A vigorous example of this style of warfare is quoted by Mr. Tyler in his "Literature of the American Revolution," and which, written in seventeen hundred and seventy-six, is entitled "The Congress." It begins:

"These hardy knaves and stupid fools,
Some apish and pragmatic mules,
Some servile acquiescing tools,—
These, these compose the Congress!"[†]

Or, again, such taunts over the general poverty of the land and character of the army as were made in a ballad called "The Rebels" by a Loyalist officer:

"With loud peals of laughter, your sides,
Sirs, would crack,
To see General Convict and Colonel Shoe-black,
With their hunting-shirts and rifle-guns,
See Cobblers and quacks, rebel priests and the like,
Pettifoggers and barbers, with sword and with pike."

Those Loyalists who lived through this exciting period in America's history bore their full share in the heavy personal misfortunes of their political party. The hatred felt toward such colonials as were true to the king has until recently hardly subsided sufficiently to permit any sympathy with the hardships they suffered. Driven from their homes, crowded together in those places occupied by the English, or exiled

* Tyler, *Literature of the American Revolution*, vol. ii, p. 182.

† *Ibid.*, p. 156.

to England or Halifax, these faithful subjects had also to undergo separation of families perhaps never again united.

Such a Loyalist was James Murray. Forced to leave his daughter and grandchildren in Boston with a sister, he took ship for Halifax to seek a living. There, amid the pressing anxieties occasioned by this separation, he strove to reëstablish himself, and sent from time to time such articles as he felt were necessary for their welfare. Thus he writes a memorandum of articles sent in seventeen hundred and eighty by "Mr. Bean's Cartel to Miss Betsy Murray:—viz: Everlasting 4 yards; binding 1 piece, Nankeen 4⅞ yards. Of Gingham 2 gown patterns; 2 pairs red shoes from A. E. C. for boys, Jack and Ralph, a parcel—to Mrs. Brigden, 1 pair silk shoes and some flowers—Arthur's Geographical Grammar, —Locke on Education,—5 children's books," etc. And in return he is informed that "Charlotte goes to dancing and writing school, improves apace and grows tall. Betsy and Charles are much better but not well. The rest of the children are in good health, desiring their duty to their Uncle and Aunt Inman, and thanks for their cake and gloves."

To such families the end of the war meant either the necessity for making permanent their residence in the British dominion, or of bearing both outspoken and silent scorn in the new Republic.

For the Americans the peace of Yorktown brought joy, but new beginnings had also to be made. Farms had been laid waste, or had suffered from lack of men to cultivate them; industries were almost at a standstill from want of material and laborers. Still the people had the splendid compensation of freedom with victory, and men went sturdily back to their homes to take up as far as possible their various occupations.

An example of the way in which business undertaken before the war was rapidly resumed, or increased, is afforded by the revival of prosperity for the booksellers in Boston, New York, and Philadelphia. Renewals of orders to London agents were speedily made, for the Americans still looked to England for their intellectual needs. In Philadelphia—a town of forty thousand inhabitants in seventeen hundred and eighty-three—among the principal booksellers and printers were Thomas Bradford, Mr. Woodhouse, Mr. Oswald, Mr. Pritchard,—who had established a circulating library,—Robert Aitkin, Mr. Liddon, Mr. Dunlap, Mr. Rice, William and David Hall, Benjamin Bache, J. Crukshank, and Robert Bell. Bell had undoubtedly the largest bookstore, but seems not to have been altogether popular, if an allusion in "The Philadelphiad" is to be credited. This "New Picture of the City" was anonymously published in seventeen hundred and eighty-four, and described, among other well-known places, Robert Bell's book-shop:

BELL'S BOOK STORE

Juſt by St. Paul's where dry divines rehearſe,
Bell keeps his ſtore for vending proſe and verſe,
And books that's neither . . . for no age nor clime,
Lame languid proſe begot on hobb'ling rhyme.
Here authors meet who ne'er a ſpring have got,
The poet, player, doctor, wit and ſot,
Smart politicians wrangling here are ſeen,
Condemning Jeffries or indulging ſpleen.

In 1776 Bell's facilities for printing had enabled him to produce an edition of "Little Goody Two-Shoes," which seems likely to have been the only story-book printed during the troubled years of the Revolution. Besides this, Bell printed in 1777 "Aesop's Fables," as did also Robert Aitkin; and J. Crukshank had issued during the war an A B C book, written by the old schoolmaster, A. Benezet, who had drilled many a Philadelphian in his letters. After the Revolution Benjamin Bache apparently printed children's books in considerable quantities, and orders were sent by other firms to England for juvenile reading-matter.

New England also has records of the sale of these small books in several towns soon after peace was established. John Carter, "at Shakespeare's Head," in Providence, announced by a broadside issued in November, seventeen hundred and eighty-three, that he had a large assortment of stationers' wares, and included in his list "Gilt Books for *Children*," among which were most of Newbery's publications. In Hartford, Connecticut, where there had been a good press since seventeen hundred and sixty-four, "The Children's Magazine" was reprinted in seventeen hundred and eighty-nine. Its preposterous titles are noteworthy, since it is probable that this was the first attempt at periodical literature made for young people in America. One number contains:

An easy Introduction to Geography.
The Schoolboy addressed to the Editors.
Moral Tales continued.
  Tale VIII. The Jealous Wife.
The Affectionate Sisters.

Familiar Letters on Various Subjects,—Continued. . . .
Letter V from *Phillis Flowerdale* to *Miss Truelove.*
Letter VI from *Miss Truelove* to *Phillis Flowerdale.*
Poetry.—The Sweets of May.
The Cottage Retirement.
Advice to the Fair.
The Contented Cottager.
The Tear.
The Honest Heart.

The autograph of Eben Holt makes the contents of the magazine ludicrous as subjects of interest to a boy But having nothing better, Eben most surely read it from cover to cover.

In Charleston, South Carolina, Robert Wells imported the books read by the members of the various branches of the Ravenel, Pinckney, Prioleau, Drayton, and other families. Boston supplied the juvenile public largely through E. Battelle and Thomas Andrews, who were the agents for Isaiah Thomas, the American Newbery.

An account of the work of this remarkable printer of Worcester, Massachusetts, has been given in Dr. Charles L. Nichols's "Bibliography of Worcester." Thomas's publications ranked as among the very best of the last quarter of the eighteenth century, and were sought by book-dealers in the various states. At one time he had sixteen presses, seven of which were in Worcester. He had also four bookstores in various towns of Massachusetts, one in Concord, New Hampshire, one in Baltimore, and one in Albany.

In 1761, at the age of ten, Thomas had set up as his "'Prentice's Token," a primer issued by A. Barclay in Cornhill, Boston, entitled "Tom Thumb's Play-Book, To Teach

Children their letters as soon as they can speak." Although this primer was issued by Barclay, Thomas had already served four years in a printer's office, for according to his own statement he had been sent at the age of six to learn his trade of Zechariah Fowle. Here, as 'prentice, he may have helped to set up the stories of the "Holy Jesus" and the "New Gift," and upon the cutting of their rude illustrations perhaps took his first lessons in engraving. For we know that by seventeen hundred and sixty-four he did fairly good work upon the "Book of Knowledge" from the press of the old printer. Upon the fly-leaf of a copy of this owned by the American Antiquarian Society, founded by Thomas, is the statement in the Worcester printer's handwriting, "Printed and cuts engraved by I. Thomas then 13 years of age for Z. Fowle when I. T. was his Apprentice: bad as the cuts are executed, there was not at that time an artist in Boston who could have done them much better. Some time before, and soon after there were better engravers in Boston." These cuts, especially the frontispiece representing a boy with a spy-glass and globe, and with a sextant at his feet, are far from poor work for a lad of thirteen. "The battered dictionary," says Dr. Nichols, "and the ink-stained Bible which he found in Fowle's office started him in his career, and the printing-press, together with an invincible determination to excel in his calling, carried him onward, until he stands to-day with Franklin and Baskerville, a type of the man who with few educational advantages succeeds because he loves his art for his art's sake."

In supplying to American children a home-made library,

Thomas, although he did no really original work for children, such as his English prototype, Newbery, had accomplished, yet had a motive which was not altogether selfish and pecuniary. The prejudice against anything of British manufacture was especially strong in the vicinity of Boston; and it was an altogether natural expression of this spirit that impelled the Worcester printer, as soon as his business was well established, to begin to reprint the various little histories. These reprints were all pirated from Newbery and his successors, Newbery and Carnan; but they compare most favorably with them, and so far surpassed the work of any other American printer of children's books (except possibly those of Bache in Philadelphia) that his work demands more than a passing mention.

Beginning, like most printers, with the production of a primer in seventeen hundred and eighty-four, by seventeen hundred and eighty-six Thomas was well under way in his work for children. In that year at least eleven little books bore his imprint and were sent to his Boston agents to be sold. In the "Worcester Magazine" for June, 1786, Thomas addressed an "Advertisement to Booksellers," as follows: "A large assortment of all the various sizes of CHILDREN'S Books, known by the name of Newbery's Little Books for Children, are now republished by I. Thomas in Worcester, Massachusetts. They are all done excellently in his English Method, and it is supposed the paper, printing, cuts, and binding are in every way equal to those imported from England. As the Subscriber has been at great expense to carry on this particular branch of Printing extensively, he hopes to meet with encouragement from the Booksellers in the United States."

Evidently he did meet with great encouragement from parents as well as booksellers; and it is suspected that the best printed books bearing imprints of other booksellers were often printed in Worcester and bound according to the taste and facilities of the dealer. That this practice of reprinting the title-page and rebinding was customary, a letter from Franklin to his nephew in Boston gives indisputable evidence:

Philada. Nov. 26, 1788.

LOVING COUSIN:

I have lately set up one of my grand-children, Benja. F. Bache, as a Printer here, and he has printed ſome very pretty little Books for Children. By the Sloop Friendſhip, Capt. Stutſon, I have ſent a Box addreſs'd to you, containing 150 of each volume, in Sheets, which I requeſt you would, according to your wonted Goodneſs, put in a way of being dispos'd of for the Benefit of my dear Sister. They are ſold here, bound in marbled Paper at 1 S. a Volume; but I ſhould ſuppoſe it beſt, if it may be done, to ſell the whole to some Stationer, at once, unbound as they are; in which caſe I imagine that half a Dollar a Quire may be thought a reaſonable Price, allowing uſual Credit if neceſsary.

My Love to your Family, & believe me ever,

Your affectionate Uncle

B. FRANKLIN.

JONA. WILLIAMS, ESQ.

Franklin's reference to the Philadelphia manner of binding toy-books in marbled paper indicates that this home-made product was already displacing the attractive imported gilt embossed and parti-colored covers used by Thomas, who seems never to have adopted this ugly dress for his juvenile publications. As the demand for his wares increased, Thomas set up other volumes from Newbery's stock, until by seventeen hundred and eighty-seven he had reproduced practically every item for his increasing trade. It was his custom to include in many of these books a Catalogue of the various tales for sale, and in "The Picture Exhibition" we find a list of fifty-two stories to be sold for prices varying from six pence to a shilling and a half.

These books may be divided into several classes, all imitations of the English adult literature then in vogue. The alphabets and primers, such as the "Little Lottery Book," "Christmas Box," and "Tom Thumb's Play-thing," are outside the limits of the present subject, since they were written primarily to instruct; and while it is often difficult to draw the line where amusement begins and instruction sinks to the background, the title-pages can usually be taken as evidence at least of the author's intention. These other books, however, fall naturally under the heads of jest and puzzle books, nature stories, fables, rhymes, novels, and stories—all prototypes of the nursery literature of to-day.

The jest and joke books published by Thomas numbered, as far as is known to the writer, only five. Their titles seem to offer a feast of fun unfulfilled by the contents. "Be Merry & Wise, or the Cream of the Jests and the Marrow of Maxims," by Tommy Trapwit, contained concentrated extracts of wisdom, and jokes such as were current among adults. The chil-

BOOKS, *for* Maſters *and* Miſſes *of all Ages, which will make them wiſe and happy, printed and ſold by* ISAIAH THOMAS, *at his* Bookſtore *in* Worceſter, *Maſſachuſetts, all ornamented with Cuts, and prettily bound.*

The following are all price four Cents each, or four federal coppers, viz.

NURSE TRUELOVE's Chriſtmas Box.

The FATHER's GIFT; or the Way to be wiſe.

The BROTHER's GIFT; or the naughty Girl reformed.

The SISTER's GIFT; or the naughty Boy reformed.

The little PUZZLING CAP; or a Collection of pretty Riddles.

The ROYAL ALPHABET; or Child's beſt Inſtructor; to which is added, the Hiſtory of a little Boy found under a Haycock.

The Death and Burial of COCK ROBBIN; with the tragical Death of A, Apple Pye.

A page from a Catalogue of Children's Books printed by Isaiah Thomas

dren for whom they were meant were accustomed to nothing more facetious than the following jest: "An arch wag said, *Taylors* were like *Woodcocks* for they got their substance by their long bills." Perhaps they understood also the point in this: "A certain lord had a termagant wife, and at the same time a chaplain that was a tolerable poet, whom his lordship desired to write a copy of verses upon a shrew. I can't imagine, said the chaplain, why your lordship should want a copy, who has so good an original." Other witticisms are not quotable.

Conundrums played their part in the eighteenth century juvenile life, much as they do to-day. These were to be found in "A Bag of Nuts ready Cracked," and "The Big and Little Puzzling Caps." "Food for the Mind" was the solemn title of another riddle-book, whose conundrums are very serious matters. Riddle XIV of the "Puzzling Cap" is typical of its rather dreary contents:

> "There was a man bespoke a thing,
> Which when the maker home did bring,
> This same maker did refuse it;
> He who bespoke it did not use it
> And he who had it did not know
> Whether he had it, yea or no."

This was a nut also "ready cracked" by the answer reproduced in the illustration.

Nature stories were attempted under the titles of "The Natural History of Four Footed Beasts," "Jacky Dandy's Delight; or the History of Birds and Beasts in Verse and Prose," "Mr. Telltruth's Natural History of Birds," and "Tommy Trip's History of Beasts and Birds." All these were written after Oliver Goldsmith's "Animated Nature" had won its way into great popularity. As a consequence of the favorable impression this book had made, Goldsmith is supposed to have been asked by Newbery to try his hand upon a juvenile natural history.

Possibly it was as a result of Newbery's request that we have the anonymous "Jacky Dandy's Delight" and "Tommy Trip's History of Beasts and Birds." The former appears to be a good example of Goldsmith's facility for amusing himself when doing hack-work for Newbery. How like Goldsmith's manner is this description of a monkey:

"The monkey mischievous
Like a naughty boy looks;
Who plagues all his friends,
And regards not his books.

"He is an active, pert, busy animal, who mimicks human actions so well that some think him rational. The Indians say, he can speak if he pleases, but will not lest he should be set to work. Herein he resembles those naughty little boys who will not learn A, lest they should be obliged to learn B, too. He is a native of warm countries, and a useless beast in this part of the world; so I shall leave him to speak of another that is more bulky, and comes from cold countries: I mean the Bear."

To poke fun in an offhand manner at little boys and girls seemed to have been the only conception of humor to be found in the children's books of the period, if we except the "Jests" and the attempts made in a ponderous manner on the title-pages. The title of "The Picture Exhibition; containing the Original Drawings of Eighteen Disciples. . . . Published under the Inspection of Mr. Peter Paul Rubens, . . ." is evidently one of Newbery's efforts to be facetious. To the author, the pretence that the pictures were by "Disciples of Peter Paul Rubens" evidently conveyed the same idea of wit that "Punch" has at times represented to others of a later century.

Fables have always been a mine of interest to young folks, and were interspersed liberally with all moral tales, but "Entertaining Fables" bears upon its title-page a suggestion that the children's old friend, "Aesop," appeared in a new dress.

Another series of books contained the much abridged novels written for the older people. "Peregrine Pickle" and "Roderick Random" were both reprinted by Isaiah Thomas as early as seventeen hundred and eighty-eight. These tales of adventure seem to have had their small reflections in such stories as "The Adventures of a Pincushion," and "The Adventures of a Peg-top," by Dorothy Kilner, an Englishwoman. Mention has already been made of "Pamela" and "Clarissa" in condensed form. These were books of over two hundred pages; but most of the toy-books were limited to less than one hundred. A remarkable instance of the pith of a long plot put into small compass was "The History of Tom Jones." A dog-eared copy of such an edition of "Tom Jones" is still in existence. Its flowery Dutch binding covers only thirty-one pages, four inches long, with a frontispiece and five wood-cut illustrations. In so small a space no detailed account of the life of the hero is to be expected; nevertheless, the first paragraph introduces Tom as no ordinary foundling. Mr. Allworthy finds the infant in his bed one evening and rings up his housekeeper Mrs. Deborah Wilkins. "She being a strict observer of decency was exceedingly alarmed, on entering her master's room, to find him undressed, but more so on his presenting her with the child, which he ordered immediately to be taken care of." The story proceeds—with little punctuation to enable the reader to take breath—to tell how the infant is named, and how Mr. Allworthy's nephew, Master Bilfil, is also brought under that generous and respectable gentleman's protection. Tommy turned out "good," as Mr. Allworthy had hoped when he assumed charge of him; and therefore eventually inherited riches and gained the hand of Miss Sophia Western, with whom he rode about the country in their "Coach and Six."

Of the stories in this juvenile library, the names, at least, of "Giles Gingerbread," "Little King Pippin," and "Goody Two-Shoes" have been handed down through various generations. One hundred years ago every child knew that "Little King Pippin" attained his glorious end by attention to his books in the beginning of his career; that "Giles Gingerbread" first learned his alphabet from gingerbread letters, and later obtained the patronage of a fine gentleman by spelling "apple-pye" correctly. Thus did his digestion prove of material assistance in mental gymnastics.

But the nursery favorite was undoubtedly "Margery, or Little Goody Two-Shoes." She was introduced to the reader in her "state of rags and care," from which she gradually emerged in the chapters entitled, "How and about Little Margery and

30 The Puzzling-Cap.

A COFFIN.

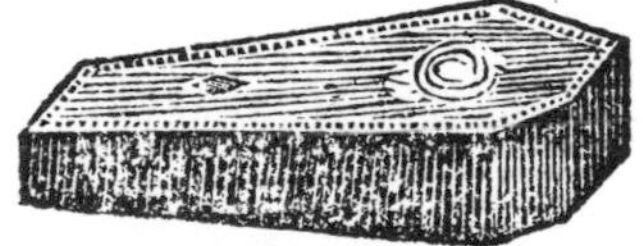

Illustration of Riddle XIV in "The Puzzling-Cap"

her Brother;" "How Little Margery obtained the name of Goody Two-Shoes;" "How she became a Tutoress" to the farmers' families in which she taught spelling by a game; and how they all sang the "Cuz's Chorus" in the intervals between the spelling lesson and the composition of sentences like this: "I pray God to bless the whole country, and all our friends and all our enemies." Like the usual heroine of eighteenth century fiction, she married a title, and as Lady Jones was the Lady Bountiful of the district. From these tales it is clear that piety as the chief end of the story-book child has been succeeded by learning as the desideratum; yet morality is still pushed into evidence, and the American mother undoubtedly translated the ethical sign-boards along the progress of the tale into Biblical admonitions.

All the books were didactic in the extreme. A series of four, called "The Mother's," "Father's," "Sister's," and "Brother's Gifts," is a good example of this didactic method of story-telling. "The Father's Gift" has lessons in spelling preceded by these lines:

"Let me not join with those in Play,
Who fibs and stories tell,
I with my Book will spend the Day,
And not with such Boys dwell.
For one rude Boy will spoil a score
As I have oft been told;
And one bad sheep, in Time, is sure
To injure all the Fold."

"The Mother's Gift" was confined largely to the same instructive field, but had one or two stories which conformed to the sentiment of the author of "The Adventures of a Pincushion," who stated her motive to be "That of providing the young reader with a few pages which should be innocent of corrupting if they did not amuse."

"The Brother's" and "Sister's Gifts," however, adopt a different plan of instruction. In "The Brother's Gift" we find a brother solicitous concerning his sister's education: "Miss Kitty Bland was apt, forward and headstrong; and had it not been for the care of her brother, Billy, would have probably witnessed all the disadvantages of a modern education"! Upon Kitty's return from boarding-school, "she could neither read, nor sew, nor write grammatically, dancing stiff and awkward, her musick inelegant, and everything she did bordered strongly on affectation." Here was a large field for reformation for Billy to effect. He had no doubts as to what method to pursue. She was desired to make him twelve shirts, and when the first one was presented to him, "he was astonished to find her lacking in so useful a female accomplishment." Exemplary conversation produced such results that the rest of the garments were satisfactory to the critical Billy, who, "as a mark of approbation made her a present of a fine pair of stays."

"The Sister's Gift" presents an opposite picture. In this case it is Master Courtley who, a "youth of Folly and Idleness," received large doses of advice from his sister. This counsel was so efficient with Billy's sensitive nature that before the story ends, "he wept bitterly, and declared to his sister that she had painted the enormity of his vices in such striking colors, that they shocked him in the greatest degree; and promised ever after to be as remarkable for generosity, compassion and every other virtue as he had hitherto been for cruelty, forwardness and ill-nature." Virtue in this instance was its own reward, as Billy received no gift in recognition of his changed habits.

To the modern lover of children such tales seem strangely ill-suited to the childish mind, losing, as they do, all tenderness in the effort of the authors (so often confided to parents in the preface) "to express their sentiments with propriety." Such criticism of the style and matter of these early attempts to write for little people was probably not made by either infant or adult readers of that old-time public. The children read what was placed before them as intellectual food, plain and sweetened, as unconcernedly as they ate the food upon their plates at meal-time. That their own language was the formal one of the period is shown by such letters as the following one from Mary Wilder, who had just read "The Mother's Gift:"

Lancaster, October 9th, 1789.

HOND. MADM:

Your goodness to me I cannot express. My mind is continually crowded with your kindness. If your goodness could be rewarded, I hope God will repay you. If you remember, some time ago I read a story in "The Mother's Gift," but I hope I shall never resemble Miss Gonson. O Dear! What a thing it is to disobey one's parents. I have one of the best Masters. He gave me a sheet of paper this morning. I hope Uncle Flagg will come up. I am quite tired of looking for Betsy, but I hope she will come. When school is done keeping, I shall come to Sudbury. What a fine book Mrs.

Chapone's Letters is: My time grows short and I must make my letter short.

Your dutiful daughter,

P. W.

Nursery rhymes and jingles of these present days have all descended from song-books of the eighteenth century, entitled "Little Robin Red Breast," "A Poetical Description of Song Birds," "Tommy Thumb's Song-Book," and the famous "Melodies of Mother Goose," whose name is happily not yet relegated to the days of long ago. Two extracts from the "Poetical Description of Song Birds" will be sufficient to show how foreign to the birds familiar to American children were the descriptions:

THE BULLFINCH

This lovely bird is charming to the sight:
The back is glossy blue, the belly white,
A jetty black shines on his neck and head;
His breast is flaming with a beauteous red.

THE TWITE

Green like the Linnet it appears to sight,
And like the Linnet sings from morn till night.
A reddish spot upon his rump is seen,
Short is his bill, his feathers always clean:
When other singing birds are dull or nice,
To sing again the merry Twites entice.

Reflections of the prevailing taste of grown people for biography are suggested in three little books, of two of which the author was Mrs. Pilkington, who had already written several successful stories for young ladies. Her "Biography for Girls" contains various novelettes, in each of which the heroine lives the conventional life and dies the conventional death of the period, and receives a laudatory epitaph. They are remarkable only as being devoid of any interest. Her "Biography for Boys" does not appear to have attained the same popularity as that for girls. A third book, "The Juvenile Biographers," containing the "Lives of Little Masters and Misses," is representative of the changes made in many books by the printer to cater to that pride in the young Republic so manifest in all local literary productions. In one biography we note a Representative to the Massachusetts Assembly:

"As Master Sammy had always been a very sober and careful child, and very attentive to his Books, it is no wonder that he proved, in the End, to be an excellent Scholar.

"Accordingly, when he had reached the age of fourteen, Mr. William Goodall, a wealthy merchant in the city of Boston, took him into his counting house, in order to bring him up in the merchantile Way, and thereby make his Fortune.

"This was a sad Stroke to his poor Sister Nancy, who having lost both her Papa and Mama, was now likely to lose her Brother likewise; but Sammy did all he could to appease her, and assured her, that he would spend all his leisure Time with her. This he most punctually performed, and never were Brother and Sister as happy in each other's company as they were.

"Mr. William Goodall was highly satisfied with Sammy's Behaviour, and dying much about the Time that Miss Nancy was married to the Gentleman, he left all his business to Sammy, together with a large Capital to carry it on. So much is Mr. Careful esteemed (for we must now no longer call him Master Sammy) that he was chosen in the late General Election, Representative in the General Court, for one of the first Towns in New England, without the least expense to himself. We here see what are the Effects of Good Behaviour."

This adaptation of the English tale to the surroundings of the American child is often found in Thomas's reprints, and naturally, owing to his enthusiasm over the recent change in the form of government, is made wholly by political references. Therefore while the lark and the linnet still sang in songs and the cowslips were scattered throughout the nature descriptions, Master Friendly no longer rode in the Lord Mayor's coach, but was seated as a Congressman in a sedan chair, "and he looked—he looked—I do not know what he looked like, but everybody was in love with him." The engraver as well as the biographer of the recently made Representative was evidently at a loss as to his appearance, as the four dots indicating the young gentleman's features give but a blank look perhaps intended to denote amazement at his election.

The illustrations of Thomas's toy reprints should not be overlooked. The Worcester printer seems to have rewritten the "Introduction" to "Goody Two-Shoes," and at the end he affixed a "Letter from the Printer which he desires may be inserted.

SIR: I have come with your copy, and so you may return it to the Vatican, if you please; and pray tell Mr. Angelo to brush up his cuts; that in the next edition they may give us a good impression."

Goody Twoshoes.

This apology for the character of the illustrations serves as an introduction to a most interesting subject of conjecture as to the making of the cuts, and particularly as to the engraving of the frontispiece in "Goody Two-Shoes."

It will be remembered that Isaiah Thomas in his advertisement to booksellers had expressly mentioned the great expense he had incurred in bringing out the juvenile books in "the English method." But Mr. Edwin Pearson, in his delightful discussion of "Banbury Chap-Books," has also stated that the wood-cut frontispiece in the first American edition of "Goody Two-Shoes," printed by Thomas, was engraved by Bewick, the famous English illustrator. A comparison of the reproduction of the Bewick engraving in Mr. Pearson's book with the frontispiece in Thomas's edition shows so much difference that it is a matter of regret that Mr. Pearson withheld his authority for attributing to Bewick the representation of Margery Two-Shoes. Besides the inference from Thomas's letter that the poor cuts would be improved before another edition should be printed, there are several points to be observed in comparing the cuts. In the first place, the execution in the Thomas cut suggests a different hand in the use of the tools; again, the reversed position of the figure of "Goody" indicates a copy of the English original. Also the expression of Thomas's heroine, although slightly mincing, is less distressed than the British dame's, to say nothing of the variation in the fashion of the gowns. And such details as the replacing of the English landscape by the spire of a meeting-house in the distance seem to confirm the impression that the drawing was made after, but not by Bewick. In the cuts scattered throughout the text the same difference in execution and portrayal of the little schoolmistress is noticeable. Margery, upon her rounds to teach the farmers' children to spell such words as "plumb-pudding" "(and who can suppose a better?)," presents her full face in the Newbery edition, and but a three-quarter view to her American admirers.

These facts, together with the knowledge that Isaiah Thomas was a fair engraver himself, make it possible that his apology for the first impression of the tiny classic was for his own engraving, which he thought to better.

Thomas not only copied and pirated Newbery's juvenile histories, but he adopted his method of advertising by insertions in the text of these tales. For example, in "The Travels of Robinson Crusoe, Written by Himself," the little reader was told, "If you learn this Book well and are good, you can buy a larger and more complete History of Mr. Crusoe at your friend the Bookseller's in Worcester near the Court House." In "The Mother's Gift," there is described well-brought-up Miss Nugent displaying to ill-bred Miss Jones, "a pretty large collection of books neatly bound and nicely kept," all to be had of Mr. Thomas; and again Mr. Careful, in "Virtue and Vice," "presented at Christmas time to the sons and daughters of his friends, little Gilt Books to read, such as are sold at Mr. Thomas' near the Court House in Worcester."

Thomas and his son continued to send out these toy-books until their gay bindings faded away before the novelty of the printed paper covers of the nineteenth century.

CHAPTER V

1790–1800

By Washington
Great deeds were done.

The New England Primer,
New York, 1794

Line after line their wisdom flows
Page after page repeating.

T. G. HAKE

CHAPTER V

1790–1800

The Child and his Book at the End of the Century

ANY attempt to trace the slow development of the American child's story of the nineteenth century must inevitably be made through the school-books written during the previous one. Before this, English books had been adapted to the American trade. But now the continued interest in education produced text-books pervaded with the American spirit. They cannot, therefore, be ignored as sporadically in the springtime of the young Republic, they, like crocuses, thrust forward in the different states their blue and yellow covers.

Next to clergymen, schoolmasters received the veneration of the people, for learning and godliness went hand in hand. It was the schoolmaster who reinforced the efforts of the parents to make good Americans of the young folks, by compiling text-books which outsold the English ones hitherto used. In the new editions of the old "New England Primer," laudatory verse about General Washington replaced the alphabet rhyme:

"Whales in the Sea
God's Voice obey."

Proud parents thereafter heard their infants lisp:

"By Washington
Great deeds were done."

For older pupils Noah Webster's speller almost superseded Dilworth's, and his "Little Readers' Assistant" became the

First Reader of many children. Webster as schoolmaster in a country district prepared this book for his own scholars. It was printed in Hartford in seventeen hundred and ninety, and contained a list of subjects suitable for farmers' children:

I. A number of Stories mostly taken from the history of America, and adorned with Cuts.

II. Rudiments of English Grammar.

III. The Federal Catechism, being a short and easy explanation of the Constitution of the United States.

IV. General principles of Government and Commerce.

V. Farmers' Catechism containing plain rules of husbandry.

Bennington, Vermont, contributed in "The Little Scholar's Pretty Pocket Companion in Rhyme and Verse," this indirect allusion to political affairs:

"'T was a toy of royalty, of late almost forgot,
'T is said she represented France
On English Monarchies arms,
But lately broke his chains by chance
And widely spread alarms."

But the most naïve attempt to inculcate patriotism together with a lesson in obedience is found in "The Child's Instructor," published about seventeen hundred and ninety-one, and written by a Philadelphian. Philadelphia had become the residence of the President—a fact that may account for one of the stories in this book about an infant prodigy called Billy. "The child at five years of age was always good and obedient, and prone to make such a remark as, 'If you would be wise you must always attend to your vowels and consonants.' When General Washington came to town Billy's mama asked him to say a speech to the ladies, and he began, 'Americans! place constantly before your eyes, the deplorable scenes of your servitude, and the enchanting picture of your deliverance. Begin with the infant in his cradle; let the first word he lisps be *Washington*.' The ladies were all delighted to hear Billy speak so well. One said he should be a lawyer, and another said he should be President of the United States. But Billy said he could not be either unless his mama gave him leave."*

Another Philadelphian attempted to embody political sentiment in "A Tale—The Political Balance; or, The Fate of Britain and America Compared." This juvenile has long since disappeared, but it was advertised by its printer, Francis Bailey, in seventeen hundred and ninety-two, together with "The History of the Little Boy found under a Haycock," and several other books for children. One year later a "History of the American Revolution" for children was also printed in Philadelphia for the generation who had been born since the war had ended. This was written in the Biblical phraseology introduced and made popular by Franklin in his famous "Parable against Persecution."

This enthusiasm over the results of the late war and scorn for the defeated English sometimes indeed cropped out in the Newbery reprints. An edition (1796) of "Goody Two-Shoes" contains this footnote in reference to the tyranny of the English landlord over Goody's father:

"*Such is the state of things in Britain. AMERICANS prize your liberty, guard your rights and be happy.*"†

* Miss Hewins, *Atlantic Monthly*, vol. lxi, p. 112.

† Brynberg. Wilmington, 1796.

In this last decade of the century that had made a nation of the colonial commonwealths, the prosperity of the country enabled more printers to pirate the generally approved Newbery library. Samuel Hall in Boston, with a shop near the court-house, printed them all, using at times the dainty covers of flowery Dutch or gilt paper, and again another style of binding occasionally used in England. "The Death and Burial of Cock Robin," for instance, has a quaint red and gilt cover, which according to Mr. Charles Welsh was made by stamping paper with dies originally used for printing old German playing-cards. He says: "To find such a cover can only be accounted for by the innocence of the purchasers as to the appearance of his Satanic Majesty's picture cards and hence [they] did not recognize them." In one corner of the book cover is impressed the single word "Münch," which stamps this paper as "made in Germany." Hall himself was probably as ignorant of the original purpose of the picture as the unsuspecting purchaser, who would cheerfully have burned it rather than see such an instrument of the Devil in the hands of its owner, little Sally Barnes.

Of Samuel Hall's reprints from the popular English publications, "Little Truths" was in all probability one of the most salable. So few books contained any information about America that one of these two volumes may be regarded as of particular interest to the young generation of his time. The author of "Little Truths," William Darton, a Quaker publisher in London, does not divulge from what source he gleaned his knowledge. His information concerning Ameri-

FRONTISPIECE.

S^r. Walter Raleigh and his man.

cans is of that misty description that confuses Indians ("native Americans") with people of Spanish and English descent. The usual "Introduction" states that "The author has chose a method after the manner of conversations between children and their instructor," and the dialogue is indicated by printing the children's observations in italics. These volumes were issued for twenty years after they were introduced by Hall, and those of an eighteen hundred Philadelphia edition are bound separately. Number one is in blue paper with copper-plate pictures on both covers. This volume gives information regarding farm produce, live-stock, and about birds quite unfamiliar to American children. But the second volume, in white covers, introduces the story of Sir Walter Raleigh and his pipe-smoking incident, made very realistic in the copper-plate frontispiece. The children's question, "*Did Sir Walter Raleigh find out the virtues of tobacco?*" affords an excellent opportunity for a discourse upon smoking and snuff-taking. These remarks conclude with this prosaic statement: "Hundreds of sensible people have fell into these customs from example; and, when they would have left them off, found it a very great difficulty." Next comes a lesson upon the growth of tobacco leading up to a short account of the slave-trade, already a subject of differing opinion in the United States, as well as in England. Of further interest to small Americans was a short tale of the discovery of this country. Perhaps to most children their first book-knowledge of this event came from the pages of "Little Truths."

Hall's books were not all so proper for the amusement of young folks. A perusal of "Capt. Gulliver's Adventures" leaves one in no doubt as to the reason that so many of the old-fashioned mothers preferred to keep such tales out of children's hands, and to read over and over again the adventures of the Pilgrim, Christian. Mrs. Eliza Drinker of Philadelphia in seventeen hundred and ninety-six was re-reading for the third time "Pilgrim's Progress," which she considered a "generally approved book," although then "ridiculed by many." The "Legacy to Children" Mrs. Drinker also read aloud to her grandchildren, having herself "wept over it between fifty and sixty years ago, as did my grandchildren when it was read to them. She, Hannah Hill, died in 1714, and ye book was printed in 1714 by Andrew Bradford."

But Mrs. Drinker's grandchildren had another book very different from the pious sayings of the dying Hannah. This contained "64 little stories and as many pictures drawn and written by Nancy Skyrin," the mother of some of the children. P. Widdows had bound the stories in gilt paper, and it was so prized by the family that the grandmother thought the fact of the recovery of the book, after it was supposed to have been irretrievably lost, worthy of an entry in her journal. Careful inquiry among the descendants of Mrs. Drinker has led to the belief that these stories were read out of existence many years ago. What they were about can only be imagined. Perhaps they were incidents in the lives of the same children who cried over the pathetic morbidity of Hannah's dying words; or possibly rhymes and verses about school and play hours of little Philadelphians; with pictures showing bait-the-bear, trap-ball, and other sports of days long since

Foot Ball

passed away, as well as "I Spie Hi" and marbles, familiar still to boys and girls.

From the fact that these stories were written for the author's own children, another book, composed less than a century before, is brought to mind. Comparison of even the meagre description of Mrs. Skyrin's book with Cotton Mather's professed purpose in "Good Lessons" shows the stride made in children's literature to be a long one. Yet a quarter of a century was still to run before any other original writing was done in America for children's benefit.

Nobody else in America, indeed, seems to have considered the question of writing for nursery inmates. Mrs. Barbauld's "Easy Lessons for Children from Two to Five Years old," written for English children, were considered perfectly adapted to gaining knowledge and perhaps amusement. It is true that when Benjamin Bache of Philadelphia issued "Easy Lessons," he added this note: "Some alterations were thought necessary to be made in this . . . American edition, to make it agree with the original design of rendering instruction easy and useful. . . . The climate and the familiar objects of this country suggested these alterations." Except for the substitution of such words as "Wheat" for "Corn," the intentions of the editor seem hardly to have had result, except by way of advertisement; and are of interest merely because they represent one step further in the direction of Americanizing the story-book literature.

All Mrs. Barbauld's books were considered excellent for young children. As a "Dissenter," she gained in the esteem of the people of the northern states, and her books were imported as well as reprinted here. Perhaps she was best known to our grandparents as the joint author, with Dr. Aikin, of "Evenings at Home," and of "Hymns in Prose and Verse." Both were read extensively for fifty years. The "Hymns" had an enormous circulation, and were often full of fine rhythm and undeserving of the entire neglect into which they have fallen. Of course, as the fashion changed in the "approved" type of story, Mrs. Barbauld suffered criticism. "Mrs. and Miss Edgeworth in their 'Practical Education' insisted that evil lurked behind the phrase in 'Easy Lessons,' 'Charles wants his dinner' because of the implication 'that Charles must have whatever he desires,' and to say 'the sun has gone to bed,' is to incur the odium of telling the child a falsehood." *

But the manner in which these critics of Mrs. Barbauld thought they had improved upon her method of story-telling is a tale belonging to another chapter. When Miss Edgeworth's wave of popularity reached this country Mrs. Barbauld's ideas still flourished as very acceptable to parents.

A contemporary and rival writer for the English nursery was Mrs. Sarah Trimmer. Her works for little children were also credited with much information they did not give. After the publication of Mrs. Barbauld's "Easy Lessons" (which was the result of her own teaching of an adopted child), Mrs. Trimmer's friends urged her to make a like use of the lessons given to her family of six, and accordingly she published in seventeen hundred and seventy-eight an "Easy Introduction into the Knowledge of Nature," and followed it some years after its initial success by "Fabulous Histories,"

* Miss Repplier, *Atlantic Monthly*, vol. lvii, p. 509.

afterwards known as the "History of the Robins." Although Mrs. Trimmer represents more nearly than Mrs. Barbauld the religious emotionalism pervading Sunday-school libraries, —in which she was deeply interested,—the work of both these ladies exemplifies the transitional stage to that Labor-in-Play school of writing which was to invade the American nursery in the next century when Parley and Abbott throve upon the proceeds of the educational narrative.

Defoe's "Robinson Crusoe" and Thomas Day's "Sanford and Merton" occupied the place in the estimation of boys that the doings of Mrs. Barbauld's and Mrs. Trimmer's works held in the opinion of the younger members of the nursery. Edition followed upon edition of the adventures of the famous island hero. In Philadelphia, in seventeen hundred and ninety-three, William Young issued what purported to be the sixth edition. In New York many thousands of copies were sold, and in eighteen hundred and twenty-four we find a Spanish translation attesting its widespread favor. In seventeen hundred and ninety-four, Isaiah Thomas placed the surprising adventures of the mariner as on the "Coast of America, lying near the mouth of the great river Oroonoque."

Parents also thought very highly of Thomas Day's "Children's Miscellany" and "Sanford and Merton." To read this last book is to believe it to be possibly in the style that Dr. Samuel Johnson had in mind when he remarked to Mrs. Piozzi that "the parents buy the books but the children never read them." Yet the testimony of publishers of the past is that "Sanford and Merton" had a large and continuous sale for many years. "'Sanford and Merton,'" writes Mr. Julian

Hawthorne, "ran 'Robinson Crusoe' harder than any other work of the eighteenth century particularly written for children." "The work," he adds, "is quaint and interesting rather to the historian than to the general, especially the child, reader. Children would hardly appreciate so amazingly ancient a form of conversation as that which resulted from Tommy [the bad boy of the story] losing a ball and ordering a ragged boy to pick it up:

"'Bring my ball directly!'

"'I don't choose it,' said the boy.

"'Sirrah,' cried Tommy, 'if I come to you I will make you choose it.'

"'Perhaps not, my pretty master,' said the boy.

"'You little rascal,' said Tommy, who now began to be very angry, 'if I come over the hedge I will thrash you within an inch of your life.'"

The gist of Tommy's threat has often been couched in modern language by grandsons of the boys from whom the Socratic Mr. Day wrote to expose the evils of too luxurious an education. His method of compilation of facts to be taught may best be given in the words of his Preface: "All who have been conversant in the education of very young children, have complained of the total want of proper books to be put in their hands, while they are taught the elements of reading. . . . The least exceptional passages of books that I could find for the purpose were 'Plutarch's Lives' and Xenophon's 'History of the Institution of Cyrus,' in English translation; with some part of 'Robinson Crusoe,' and a few passages from Mr. Brooke's 'Fool of Quality.' . . . I therefore resolved . . .

not only to collect all such stories as I thought adapted to the faculties of children, but to connect these by continued narration. . . . As to the histories themselves, I have used the most unbounded licence. . . . As to the language, I have endeavored to throw into it a greater degree of elegance and ornament than is usually to be met with in such compositions; preserving at the same time a sufficient degree of simplicity to make it intelligible to very young children, and rather choosing to be diffuse than obscure." With these objects in mind, we can understand small Tommy's embellishment of his demand for the return of his ball by addressing the ragged urchin as "Sirrah."

Mr. Day's "Children's Miscellany" contained a number of stories, of which one, "The History of Little Jack," about a lost child who was adopted by a goat, was popular enough to be afterwards published separately. It is a debatable question as to whether the parents or the children figuring in this "Miscellany" were the more artificial. "Proud and unfeeling girl," says one tender mother to her little daughter who had bestowed half her pin money upon a poor family,—"proud and unfeeling girl, to prefer vain and trifling ornaments to the delight of relieving the sick and miserable! Retire from my presence! Take away with you trinket and nosegay, and receive from them all the comforts they are able to bestow!" Why Mr. Day's stories met with such unqualified praise at the time they were published, this example of canting rubbish does not reveal. In real life parents certainly did retain some of their substance for their own pleasure; why, therefore, discipline a child for following the same inclination?

In contrast to Mr. Day's method, Mrs. Barbauld's plan of simple conversation in words of one, two, and three syllables seems modern. Both aimed to afford pleasure to children "learning the elements of reading." Where Mrs. Barbauld probably judged truly the capacity of young children in the dialogues with the little Charles of "Easy Lessons," Mr. Day loaded his gun with flowers of rhetoric and overshot infant comprehension.

Nevertheless, in spite of the criticism that has waylaid and torn to tatters Thomas Day's efforts to provide a suitable and edifying variety of stories, his method still stands for the distinct secularization of children's literature of amusement. Moreover, as Mr. Montrose J. Moses writes in his delightful study of "Children's Books and Reading," "he foreshadowed the method of retelling incidents from the classics and from standard history and travel,—a form which is practised to a great extent by our present writers, who thread diverse materials on a slender wire of subsidiary story, and who, like Butterworth and Knox, invent untiring families of travellers who go to foreign parts, who see things, and then talk out loud about them."

Besides tales by English authors, there was a French woman, Madame de Genlis, whose books many educated people regarded as particularly suitable for their daughters, both in the original text and in the English translations. In Aaron Burr's letters we find references to his interest in the progress made by his little daughter, Theodosia, in her studies. His zeal in searching for helpful books was typical of the care many others took to place the best literature within their children's reach. From Theodosia's own letters to her father we learn that she was a studious child, who wrote and ciphered from five to eight every morning and during the same hours every evening. To improve her French, Mr. Burr took pains to find reading-matter when his law practice necessitated frequent absence from home. Thus from West Chester, in seventeen hundred and ninety-six, when Theodosia was nine years old, he wrote:

I rose up suddenly from the sofa and rubbing my head—"What book shall I buy for her?" said I to myself. "She reads so much and so rapidly that it is not easy to find proper and amusing French books for her; and yet I am so flattered with her progress in that language, that I am resolved that she shall, at all events, be gratified." So . . . I took my hat and sallied out. It was not my first attempt. I went into one bookseller's after another. I found plenty of fairy tales and such nonsense, for the generality of children of nine or ten years old. "These," said I, "will never do. Her understanding begins to be above such things." . . . I began to be discouraged. "But I will search a little longer." I persevered. At last I found it. I found the very thing I sought. It is contained in two volumes, octavo, handsomely bound, and with prints and reprints. It is a work of fancy but replete with instruction and amusement. I must present it with my own hand.

Yr. affectionate

A. Burr.

What speculation there must have been in the Burr family as to the name of the gift, and what joy when Mr. Burr presented the two volumes upon his return! From a letter written later by Mr. Burr to his wife, it appears that he afterward found reason to regret his purchase, which seems to have been Madame de Genlis's famous "Annales." "Your account," he wrote, "of Madame Genlis surprises me, and is new evidence of the necessity of reading books before we put them in the hands of children." Opinion differed, of course, concerning the French lady's books. In New York, in Miss Dodsworth's most genteel and fashionable school, a play written from "The Dove" by Madame de Genlis was acted with the same zest by little girls of ten and twelve years of age as they showed in another play taken from "The Search after Happiness," a drama by the Quakeress and religious writer, Hannah More. These plays were given at the end of school terms by fond parents with that appreciation of the histrionic ability of their daughters still to be seen on such occasions.

No such objection as Mrs. Burr made to this lady's "Annales" was possible in regard to another French book, by Berquin. Entitled "Ami des Enfans," it received under the Rev. Mr. Cooper's translation the name "The Looking Glass for the Mind." This collection of tales supposedly mirrored the frailties and virtues of rich and poor children. It was often bound in full calf, and an edition of seventeen hundred and ninety-four contains a better engraved frontispiece than it was customary to place in juvenile publications. For half a century it was to be found in the shop of all booksellers, and had its place in the library of every family of means. There are still those among us who have not forgotten the impression produced upon their infant minds by certain of the tales. Some remember the cruel child and the canary. Others recollect their admiration of the little maid who, when all others deserted her young patroness, lying ill with the smallpox, won the undying gratitude of the mother by her tender nursing. The author, blind himself to the possibilities of detriment to the sick child by unskilled care, held up to the view of all, this example of devotion of one girl in contrast to the hard-heartedness of many others. This book seems also to have been called by the literal translation of its original title, "Ami des Enfans;" for in an account of the occupations of one summer Sunday in seventeen hundred and ninety-seven, Julia Cowles, living in Litchfield, Connecticut, wrote: "Attended meeting all day long, but do not recollect the text. Read in 'The Children's Friend.'" Many children would not have been permitted to read so nearly secular a book; but evidently Julia Cowles's parents were liberal in their view of Sunday reading after the family had attended "meeting all day long."

In addition to the interest of the context of these toy-books of a past generation, one who handles such relics of a century ago sees much of the fashions for children of that day. In "The Looking Glass," for instance, the illustrations copied from engravings by the famous English artist, Bewick, show that at the end of the eighteenth century children were still clothed like their elders; the coats and waistcoats, knee breeches and hats, of boys were patterned after gentlemen's garments, and the caps and aprons, kerchiefs and gowns, for girls were reproductions of the mothers' wardrobes.

Again, the fly-leaf of "The History of Master Jacky and Miss Harriot" arrests the eye by its quaint inscription:

"Rozella Ford's Book. For being the second speller second class." At once the imagination calls up the ex in a village school at the end of a year's session: a row little maids and sturdy boys, standing before the schoo and by turn spelling in shrill tones words of three to f lables, until only two, Rozella and a better speller, unconfused by Dilworth's and Webster's word my Then the two children step forward with bow and to receive their tiny gilt prizes from a pile of duod upon the teacher's desk. Indeed, the giving of rewar carried to such an extent as to become a great drai the meagre stipend of the teacher. Thus when in coppe handwriting we find in another six-penny volume the i tion: "Benjamin H. Bailey, from one he esteems and Mr. Hapgood," we read between its lines the self-deni tised by Mr. Hapgood, who possibly received, like other teachers, but seventy-five cents a week besides hi and lodging.

Other books afford a glimpse of children's life: the every-day routine, the plays they enjoyed, and their stration of a sensibility as keen as was then in fash adults. The "History of a Doll," lying upon the table, is among the best in this respect. It was ev much read by its owner and fairly "loved to pieces." it reached this disintegrated stage, a careful mother, sewed it with coarse flax thread inside a home-mad of bright blue wall-paper. Although the "History of th igree and Rise of the Pretty Doll" bears no date, it panion story in the wall-paper wrapper has the impri enteen hundred and ninety-one, and this, together with the press-work, places it as belonging to the eighteenth century. It offers to the reader a charming insight into the formality of many an old-fashioned family: the deportment stiff with the starched customs of that day, the seriousness of their fun, and the sensibility among little maidens akin to that exhibited in the heroines of fiction created by Richardson and Fielding.

The chapter concerning "The Pedigree of the Doll" treats of finding a branch of a tree by a carver, who was desired by Sir John Amiable to make one of the best dolls in his power for his "pretty little daughter who was as good as she was pretty." The carver accordingly took the branch and began carving out the head, shoulders, body, and legs, which he soon brought to their proper shape. "He then covered it with a fine, flesh-colored enamel and painted its cheeks in the most lively manner. It had the finest black and sparkling eyes that were ever beheld; its cheeks resembled the blushing rose, its neck the lilly, and its lips the coral." The doll is presented, and the next chapter tells of "an assembly of little female gossips in full debate on the clothing of the doll." "Miss Polly having made her papa a vast number of courtesies for it, prevailed on her brother to go round to all the little gossips in the neighborhood, begging their company to tea in the afternoon, in order to consult in what mode the doll should be dressed." The company assembled. "Miss Micklin undertook to make it a fine ruffled laced shift, Miss Mantua to make it a silk sacque and petticoat; and in short, every one contributed, in some measure, to dress out this beautiful creature."

"Everything went on with great harmony till they came to the head-dress of the doll; and here they differed so much in opinion, that all their little clappers were going at once. . . . Luckily, at this instant Mrs. Amiable happened to come in, and soon brought the little gossips to order. The matter in dispute was, whether it should have a high head-dress or whether the hair should come down on the forehead, and the curls flow in natural ringlets on the shoulders. However, after some pretty warm debate, this last mode was adopted, as most proper for a little miss." In chapter third "The doll is named:—Accidents attend the Ceremony." Here we have a picture of a children's party. "The young ladies and gentlemen were entertained with tea and coffee; and when that was over, each was presented with a glass of raisin wine." During the christening ceremony an accident happened to the doll, because Master Tommy, the parson, "in endeavouring to get rid of it before the little gossips were ready to receive it, made a sad blunder. . . . Miss Polly, with tears in her eyes, snatched up the doll and clasped it to her bosom; while the rest of the little gossips turned all the little masters out of the room, that they might be left to themselves to inquire more privately into what injuries the dear doll had received. . . . Amidst these alarming considerations Tommy Amiable sent the ladies word, that, if they would permit him and the rest of the young gentlemen to pass the evening among them in the parlour, he would engage to replace the nose of the doll in such a manner that not the appearance of the late accident should be seen." Permission was accordingly granted for a surgical operation upon the nose, but "as to the fracture in one of the doll's legs, it was never certainly known how that was remedied, as the young ladies thought it very indelicate to mention anything about the matter." The misadventures of the doll include its theft by a monkey in the West Indies, and at this interesting point the only available copy of the tale is cut short by the loss of the last four pages. The charm of this book lies largely in the fact that the owner of the doll does not grow up and marry as in almost every other novelette. This difference, of course, prevents the story from being a typical one of its period, but it is, nevertheless, a worthy forerunner of those tales of the nineteenth century in which an effort was made to write about incidents in a child's life, and to avoid the biographical tendency.

Before leaving the books of the eighteenth century, one tale must be mentioned because it contains the germ of the idea which has developed into Mr. George's "Junior Republic." It was called "Juvenile Trials for Robbing Orchards, Telling Tales and other Heinous Offenses." "This," said Dr. Aikin —Mrs. Barbauld's brother and collaborator in "Evenings at Home"—"is a very pleasing and ingenious little Work, in which a Court of Justice is supposed to be instituted in a school, composed of the Scholars themselves, for the purpose of trying offenses committed at School." In "Trial the First" Master Tommy Tell-Truth charges Billy Prattle with robbing an orchard. The jury, after hearing Billy express his contrition for his act, brings in a verdict of guilty; but the judge pardons the culprit because of his repentant frame of mind. Miss Delia, the offender in case *Number Two*, does not escape so lightly. Miss Stirling charges her with raising contention and strife among her school-fellows over a piece of angelica, "whereby," say her prosecutors, "one had her favorite cap torn to pieces, and her hair which had been that day nicely dressed, pulled all about her shoulders; another had her sack torn down the middle; a third had a fine flowered apron of her own working, reduced to rags; a fourth was wounded by a pelick, or scratch of her antagonist, and in short, there was hardly one among them who had not some mark to shew of having been concerned in this unfortunate affair." That the good Dr. Aikin approved of the punishment decreed, we are sure. The little prisoner was condemned to pass three days in her room, as just penalty for such "indelicate" behaviour.

By the close of the century Miss Edgeworth was beginning to supersede Mrs. Barbauld in England; but in America the taste in juvenile reading was still satisfied with the older writer's little Charles, as the correct model for children's deportment, and with Giles Gingerbread as the exemplary student. The child's lessons had passed from "Be good or you will go to Hell" to "Be good and you will be rich;" or, with the Puritan element still so largely predominant, "Be good and you will go to Heaven." Virtue as an ethical quality had been shown in "Goody Two-Shoes" to bring its reward as surely as vice brought punishment. It is to be doubted if this was altogether wholesome; and it may well be that it was with this idea in mind that Dr. Johnson made his celebrated criticism of the nursery literature in vogue, when he said to Mrs. Piozzi, "Babies do not want to be told about babies; they like to be told of giants and castles, and of somewhat which can stretch and stimulate their little minds."*

The learned Doctor, having himself been brought up on "Jack the Giant Killer" and "The History of Blue Beard," was inclined to scorn Newbery's tales as lacking in imaginative quality. That Dr. Johnson was really interested in stories for the young people of his time is attested by a note written in seventeen hundred and sixty-three on the fly-leaf of a collection of chap-books: "I shall certainly, sometime or other, write a little Story-Book in the style of these. I shall be happy to succeed, for he who pleases children will be remembered by them."†

In America, however, it is doubtful whether any true critical spirit regarding children's books had been reached. Fortunately in England, at the beginning of the next century, there was a man who dared speak his opinion. Mrs. Barbauld and Mrs. Trimmer (who had contributed "Fabulous Histories" to the juvenile library, and for them had shared the approval which greeted Mrs. Barbauld's efforts) were the objects of Charles Lamb's particular detestation. In a letter to Coleridge, written in 1802, he said:

"Goody Two Shoes is almoſt out of print. Mrs. Barbauld's ſtuff haſ baniſhed all the old claſſics of the nurſery, and the ſhopman at Newbery's hardly deigned to reach them off an old exploded corner of a ſhelf, when Mary aſked for them. Mrs. Barbauld's and Mrs. Trimmer's nonſenſe lay in piles about. Knowledge inſignificant and vapid as Mrs. Barbauld's books convey, it ſeems, muſt come to a child in the ſhape

* Hill, *Johnsonian Miscellany*, vol. i, p. 157. † *Ibid.*

of knowledge; and hiſ empty noddle muſt be turned with conceit of hiſ own powers when he has learned that a horſe is an animal and Billy is better than a horſe, and ſuch like, inſtead of that beautiful intereſt in wild tales, which made the child a man, while all the time he ſuſpected himſelf to be no bigger than a child. Science has ſucceeded to poetry no leſs in the little walks of children than of men. Is there no poſſibility of arreſting this force of evil? Think what you would have been now, if inſtead of being fed with tales and old wives' fables in childhood, you had been crammed with geography and natural hiſtory. Hang them! I mean the curſed Barbauld crew, thoſe blights and blaſts of all that is human in man and child."*

To Lamb's extremely sensitive nature, the vanished hand of the literary man of Grub Street could not be replaced by Mrs. Barbauld's wish to instruct by using simple language. It is possible that he did her some injustice. Yet a retrospective glance over the story-book literature evolved since Newbery's juvenile library was produced, shows little that was not poor in quality and untrue to life. Therefore, it is no wonder that Lamb should have cried out against the sore evil which had "beset a child's mind." All the poetry of life, all the imaginative powers of a child, Mrs. Barbauld, Mrs. Trimmer, and Mr. Day ignored; and Newbery in his way, and the old ballads in their way, had appealed to both.

In both countries the passion for knowledge resulted in this curious literature of amusement. In England books were written; in America they were reprinted, until a religious

* Welsh, *Introduction to Goody Two Shoes*, p. x.

revival left in its wake the series of morbid and educational tales which the desire to write original stories for American children produced.

CHAPTER VI

1800–1825

Her morals then the Matron read,
Studious to teach her Children dear,
And they by love or Duty led,
With Pleasure read.

A Mother's Remarks,
Philadelphia, 1810

Mama! see what a pretty book
At Day's papa has bought,
That I may at its pictures look,
And by its words be taught.

CHAPTER VI

1800–1825

Toy-Books in the Early Nineteenth Century

ON the 23d of December, 1823, there appeared anonymously in the "Troy (New York) Sentinel," a Christmas ballad entitled "A Visit from St. Nicholas." This rhymed story of Santa Claus and his reindeer, written one year before its publication by Clement Clarke Moore for his own family, marks the appearance of a truly original story in the literature of the American nursery.

We have seen the somewhat lugubrious influence of Puritan and Quaker upon the occasional writings for American children; and now comes a story bearing upon its face the features of a Dutchman, as the jolly old gentleman enters nursery lore with his happy errand.

Up to this time children of wholly English extraction had probably little association with the Feast of St. Nicholas. The Christmas season had hitherto been regarded as pagan in its origin by people of Puritan or Scotch descent, and was celebrated only as a religious festival by the descendants of the more liberal adherents to the Church of England. The Dutch element in New York, however, still clung to some of their traditions; and the custom of exchanging simple gifts upon Christmas Day had come down to them as a result of a combination of the church legend of the good St. Nicholas, patron of children, and the Scandinavian myth of the fairy gnome, who from his bower in the woods showered good children with gifts.* But to celebrate the day quietly was altogether a different thing from introducing to the American public the character of Santa Claus, who has become in his mythical entity as well known to every American as that other Dutch legendary personage, Rip Van Winkle.

In the "Visit from St. Nicholas" Mr. Moore not only introduced Santa Claus to the young folk of the various states, but gave to them their first story of any lasting merit whatsoever. It is worthy of remark that as every impulse to write for juvenile readers has lagged behind the desire to write for adults, so the composition of these familiar verses telling of the arrival in America of the mysterious and welcome visitor on

> "The night before Christmas, when all through the house
> Not a creature was stirring, not even a mouse,"

fell at the end of that quarter of the nineteenth century to which we are accustomed to refer as the beginning of the national period of American literature.

It is, of course, true that the older children of that period had already begun to enjoy some of the writings of Irving and Cooper, and to learn the fortunately still familiar verses by Hopkinson, Key, Drake, and Halleck. School-readers have served to familiarize generation after generation with "Hail Columbia," "The Star Spangled Banner," and sometimes with "The American Flag." It is, doubtless, their authors' jubilant enthusiasm over the freedom of the young Republic that has caused the children of the more mature nation to delight in the repetition of the patriotic verses. The youth-

*As long ago as seventeen hundred and sixty-two, Garrat Noel, a Dutch bookseller in New York, advertised that, "according to his Annual Custom, he . . . provided a very large Assortment of Books . . . as proper Presents at Christmas." See page 68.

ful extravagance of expression pervading every line is re-echoed in the heart of the schoolboy, who likes to imagine himself, before anything else, a patriot. But until "Donder and Blitzen" pranced into the foreground as Santa Claus' steeds, there was nothing in American nursery literature of any lasting fame. Thereafter, as the custom of observing Christmas Day gradually became popular, the perennial small child felt—until automobiles sent reindeer to the limbo of bygone things—the thrill of delight and fear over the annual visit of Santa Claus that the bigger child experiences in exploding fire-crackers on the Fourth of July. There are possibilities in both excitements which appeal to one of the child's dearest possessions — his imagination.

It is this direct appeal to the imagination that surprises and delights us in Mr. Moore's ballad. To re-read it is to be amazed that anything so full of merriment, so modern, so free from pompousness or condescension, from pedantry or didacticism, could have been written before the latter half of the nineteenth century. Not only its style is simple in contrast with the labored efforts at simplicity of its contemporaneous verse, but its story runs fifty years ahead of its time in its freedom from the restraining hand of the moralist and from the warning finger of the religious teacher, if we except Nathaniel Hawthorne's "Wonder Book."

In our examination of the toy-books of twenty years preceding its publication, we shall find nothing so attractive in manner, nor so imaginative in conception. Indeed, we shall see, upon the one hand, that fun was held in with such a tight curb that it hardly ever escaped into print; and upon the other hand that the imagination had little chance to develop because of the prodigal indulgence in realities and in religious experience from which all authors suffered. We shall also see that these realities were made very uncompromising and uncomfortable to run counter to. Duty spelled in capital letters was a stumbling-block with which only the well-trained story-book child could successfully cope; recreation followed in small portions large shares of instruction, whether disguised or bare faced. The Religion-in-Play, the Ethics-in-Play, and the Labor-in-Play schools of writing for children had arrived in America from the land of their origin.

The stories in vogue in England during this first quarter of the nineteenth century explain every vagary in America. There fashionable and educational authorities had hitched their wagon to the literary star, Miss Edgeworth, and the followers of her system; while the religiously inclined pinned their faith also upon tracts written by Miss Hannah More. In this still imitative land the booksellers simply reprinted the more successful of these juvenile publications. The changes, therefore, in the character of the juvenile literature of amusement of the early nineteenth century in America were due to the adoption of the works of these two Englishwomen, and to the increased facilities for reproducing toy-books, both in press-work and in illustrations.

Hannah More's allegories and religious dramas, written to coöperate with the teachings of the first Sabbath Day schools, are, of course, outside the literature of amusement. Yet they affected its type in America as they undoubtedly gave direction to the efforts of the early writers for children.

Miss More, born in seventeen hundred and fifty-four, was a woman of already established literary reputation when her attention was attracted by Robert Raikes's successful experiment of opening a Sunday-school, in seventeen hundred and eighty-one. During the religious revival that attended the preaching of George Whitefield, Raikes, already interested in the hardships and social condition of the working-classes, was further aroused by his intimate knowledge of the manner of life of some children in a pin factory. To provide instruction for these child laborers, who, without work or restrictions on Sundays, sought occupation far from elevating, Raikes founded the first "Sabbath Day school."

The movement spread rapidly in England, and ten years later, in seventeen hundred and ninety-one, under the inspiration of Bishop White, the pioneer First Day school in America was opened in Philadelphia. The good Bishop was disturbed mentally by the religious and moral degeneracy of the poor children in his diocese, and annoyed during church services by their clamor outside the churches—a noise often sufficient to drown the prayers of his flock and the sermons of his clergy. To occupy these restless children for a part of the day, two sessions of the school were held each Sunday: one before the morning service, from eight until half-past ten o'clock, and the other in the afternoon for an hour and a half. The Bible was used as a reader, and the teaching was done regularly by paid instructors.

The first Sunday-school library owed its origin to a wish to further the instruction given in the school, and hence contained books thought admirably adapted to Sunday reading. Among the somewhat meagre stock provided for this purpose were Doddridge's "Power of Religion," Miss More's tracts and the writings of her imitators, together with "The Fairchild Family," by Mrs. Sherwood, "The Two Lambs," by Mrs. Cameron, "The Economy of Human Life," and a little volume made up of selections from Mrs. Barbauld's works for children. "The Economy of Human Life," said Miss Sedgwick (who herself afterwards wrote several good books for girls), "was quite above my comprehension, and I thought it unmeaning and tedious." Testimony of this kind about a book which for years appeared regularly upon booksellers' lists enables us to realize that the average intelligent child of the year eighteen hundred was beginning to be as bored by some of the literature placed in his hands as a child would be one hundred years later.

To increase this special class of books, Hannah More devoted her attention. Her forty tracts comprising "The Cheap Repository" included "The Shepherd of Salisbury Plain" and "The Two Shoemakers," which, often appearing in American booksellers' advertisements, were for many years a staple article in Sunday-school libraries, and even now, although pushed to the rear, are discoverable in some such collections of books. Their objective point is best given by their author's own words in the preface to an edition of "The Search after Happiness; A Pastoral Drama," issued by Jacob Johnson of Philadelphia in eighteen hundred and eleven.

Miss More began in the self-depreciatory manner then thought modest and becoming in women writers: "The author is sensible it may have many imperfections, but if it may be happily instrumental in producing a regard to Religion and Virtue in the minds of Young Persons, and afford them an innocent, and perhaps not altogether unuseful amusement in the exercise of recitation, the end for which it was originally composed . . . will be fully answered." A drama may seem to us above the comprehension of the poor and illiterate class of people whose attention Miss More wished to hold, but when we feel inclined to criticise, let us not forget that the author was one who had written little eight-year-old Thomas Macaulay: "I think we have nearly exhausted the epics. What say you to a little good prose? Johnson's 'Hebrides,' or Walton's 'Lives,' unless you would like a neat edition of Cowper's poems or 'Paradise Lost.'"

Miss More's influence upon the character of Sunday-school books in England undoubtedly did much to incline many unknown American women of the nineteenth century to take up this class of books as their own field for religious effort and pecuniary profit.

Contemporary with Hannah More's writings in the interest of religious life of Sunday-school scholars were some of the literary products of the painstaking pen of Maria Edgeworth.

Mention of Miss Edgeworth has already been made. About her stories for children criticism has played seriously, admiringly, and contemptuously. It is not the present purpose, however, to do other than to make clear her own aim, and to try to show the effect of her extremely moral tales upon her own generation of writers for American children. It is possible that she affected these authors more than the child audience for whom she wrote. Little ones have a wonderful faculty for seizing upon what suits them and leaving the remainder for their elders to discuss.

Maria Edgeworth's life was a long one. Born in seventeen hundred and sixty-seven, when John Newbery's books were at the height of their fame, she lived until eighteen hundred and forty-nine, when they were scarcely remembered; and now her own once popular tales have met a similar fate.

She was educated by a father filled with enthusiasm by the teachings of Rousseau and with advice from the platitudinous family friend, Thomas Day, author of "Sanford and Merton." Only the truly genial nature and strong character of Miss Edgeworth prevented her genius from being altogether swamped by this incongruous combination. Fortunately, also, her busy practical home life allowed her sympathies full sway and counteracted many of the theories introduced by Mr. Edgeworth into his family circle. Successive stepmothers filled the Edgeworth nursery with children, for whom the devoted older sister planned and wrote the stories afterward published.

In seventeen hundred and ninety-one Maria Edgeworth, at her father's suggestion, began to note down anecdotes of the children of the family, and later these were often used as copy to be criticised by the little ones themselves before they were turned over to the printer. Her father's educational conversations with his family were often committed to paper, and these also furnished material from which Miss Edgeworth made it her object in life to interweave knowledge, amusement, and ethics. Indeed, it has been most aptly said that between the narrow banks of Richard Edgeworth's theories

Jacob Johnson's Book-Store

"his daughter's genius flowed through many volumes of amusement."

Her first collection of tales was published under the title of "The Parent's Assistant," although Miss Edgeworth's own choice of a name had been the less formidable one of "The Parent's Friend." Based upon her experience as eldest sister in a large and constantly increasing family, these tales necessarily struck many true notes and gave valuable hints to perplexed parents. In "The Parent's Assistant" realities stalked full grown into the nursery as

> "Every object in creation
> Furnished hints for contemplation."

The characters were invariably true to their creator's original drawing. A good girl was good from morning to night; a naughty child began and ended the day in disobedience, and by it bottles were smashed, strawberries spilled, and lessons disregarded in unbroken sequence. In later life Miss Edgeworth confessed to having occasionally introduced in "Harry and Lucy" some nonsense as an "alloy to make the sense work well;" but as all her earlier children's tales were subjected to the pruning scissors of Mr. Edgeworth, this amalgam is to-day hardly noticeable in "Popular Tales," "Early Lessons," and "Frank," which preceded the six volumes of "Harry and Lucy."

Although a contemporary of Mrs. Barbauld, who had written for little children "Easy Lessons," Miss Edgeworth does not seem to have been well known in America until about eighteen hundred and five. Then "Harry and Lucy" was brought out by Jacob Johnson, a Philadelphia book-dealer. This was issued in six small red and blue marbled paper volumes, although other parts were not completed until eighteen hundred and twenty-three. Between the first and second parts of volume one the educational hand of Mr. Edgeworth is visible in the insertion of a "Glossary," "to give a popular meaning of the words." "This Glossary," the editor, Mr. Edgeworth, thought, "should be read to children a little at a time, and should be made the subject of conversation. Afterwards they will read it with more pleasure." The popular meaning of words may be succinctly given by one definition: "Dry, what is not wet." Could anything be more lucid?

Among the stories by Miss Edgeworth are three rarely mentioned by critics, and yet among the most natural and entertaining of her short tales. They were also printed by Jacob Johnson in Philadelphia, in eighteen hundred and five, under the simple title, "Three Stories for Children." "Little Dog Trusty" is a dog any small child would like to read about; "The Orangeman" was a character familiar to English children; and "The Cherry Orchard" is a tale of a day's pleasure whose spirit American children could readily seize. In each Miss Edgeworth had a story to tell, and she told it well, even though "she walked," as has been often said, "as mentor beside her characters."

Of Miss Edgeworth's many tales, "Waste Not, Want Not" was long considered a model. In it what Mr. Edgeworth styled the "shafts of ridicule" were aimed at the rich nephew of Mr. Gresham. Mr. Gresham (whose prototype we strongly suspect was Mr. Edgeworth himself) "lived neither in idleness nor extravagance," and was desirous of adopting an heir to his considerable property. Therefore, he invited two nephews to visit him, with the object of choosing the more suitable for his purpose; apparently he had only to signify his wish and no parental objection to his plan would be interposed. The boys arrive: Hal, whose mama spends her days at Bath over cards with Lady Diana Sweepstake, is an ill-bred child, neither deferential to his uncle, nor with appetite for buns when queen-cakes may be had. His cousin Ben, on the contrary, has been taught those virtuous habits that make for a respectful attitude toward rich uncles and assure a dissertation upon the beneficial effect of buns *versus* queen-cakes. The boys, having had their characters thus definitely shown, proceed to live up to them in every particular. From start to finish it is the virtuous Ben—his generosity, thrift, and foresight are never allowed to lapse for an instant—who triumphs in every episode. He saves his string, "good whip-cord," when requested by Mr. Gresham to untie a parcel, and it thereafter serves to spin a fine new top, to help Hal out of a difficulty with his toy, and in the final incident of the story, an archery contest, our provident hero, finding his bowstring "cracked," calmly draws from his pocket the still excellent piece of cord, and affixing it to his bow, wins the match. Hal betrays his great lack of self-control by exclaiming, "The everlasting whipcord, I declare," and thereupon Patty, Mr. Gresham's only child, who has suffered from Hal's defects of character, openly rejoices when the prize is given to Ben. As is usual with Miss Edgeworth's badly behaved children, the reader now sees the error of Hal's ways, and perceives also that in the lad's acknowledgment of the truth of the formerly scorned motto, "Waste not, want not," the era of his reformation has begun.

Perpetual action was the key to the success of Miss Edgeworth's writings. If to us her fictitious children seem like puppets whose strings are too obviously jerked, the monotonous moral cloaked in the variety of incident was liked by her own generation,

Miss Edgeworth not only pleased the children, but received the applause of their parents and friends. Sir Walter Scott, the prince of story-tellers, found much to admire in her tales, and wrote of "Simple Susan:" "When the boy brings back the lamb to the little girl, there is nothing for it but to put down the book and cry." Susan was the pattern child in the tale, "clean as well as industrious," while Barbara — a violent contrast — was conceited and lazy, and a *lady* who "could descend without shame from the height of insolent pride to the lowest measure of fawning familiarity." Therefore it is small wonder that Sir Walter passed her by without mention.

However much we may value an English author's admiration for Miss Edgeworth's story-telling gifts, it is to America that we naturally turn to seek contemporary opinion. In educational circles there is no doubt that Miss Edgeworth won high praise. That her books were not always easy to procure, however, we know from a letter written from Washington by Mrs. Josiah Quincy, whose life as a child during the Revolution has already been described. When Mrs. Quincy was living in the capital city in eighteen hundred and ten, during her husband's term as Congressman, she found it difficult to provide her family with books. She therefore wrote to Boston to a friend, requesting to have sent her Miss Edgeworth's "Moral Tales," "if the work can be obtained in one of the bookstores. If not," she continued, "borrow one . . . and I will replace it with a new copy. Cut the book out of its binding and enclose the pages in packets. . . . Be careful to send the entire text and title page." The scarcity in Washington of books for young people Mrs. Quincy thought justified the hope that reprinting these tales would be profitable to a bookseller in whose efforts to introduce a better taste among the inhabitants she took a keen interest. But Mrs. Quincy need not have sent to Boston for them. Jacob Johnson in Philadelphia had issued most of the English author's books by eighteen hundred and five, and New York publishers probably made good profit by printing them.

Reading aloud was both a pastime and an education to families in those early days of the Republic. Although Mrs. Quincy made every effort to procure Miss Edgeworth's stories for her family because, in her opinion, "they obtained a decided preference to the works of Hannah More, Mrs. Trimmer and Mrs. Chapone," for reading aloud she chose extracts from Shakespeare, Milton, Addison, and Goldsmith. Indeed, if it were possible to ask our great-grandparents what books they remembered reading in their childhood, I think we should find that beyond somewhat hazy recollections of Miss Edgeworth's books and Berquin's "The Looking Glass for the Mind," they would either mention "Robinson Crusoe," Newbery's tales of "Giles Gingerbread," "Little King Pippin," and "Goody Two-Shoes" (written fifty years before their own childhood), or remember only the classic tales and sketches read to them by their parents.

Certainly this is the case if we may take as trustworthy the recollections of literary people whose childhood was passed in the first part of the nineteenth century. Catharine Sedgwick, for instance, has left a charming picture of American family life in a country town in eighteen hundred—a life doubtless paralleled by many households in comfortable circumstances. Among the host of little prigs and prudes in story-books of the day, it is delightful to find in Catharine Sedgwick herself an example of a bookish child who was natural. Her reminiscences include an account of the way the task of sweeping out the schoolhouse after hours was made bearable by feasts of Malaga wine and raisins. These she procured from the store where her father kept an open account, until the bill having been rendered dotted over with such charges "per daughter Catharine," these treats to favorite schoolmates ceased. Also a host of intimate details of this large family's life in the country brings us in touch with the times: fifteen pairs of calfskin shoes ordered from the village shoemaker, because town-bought morocco slippers were few and far between; the excitement of a silk gown; the distress of a brother, whose trousers for fête occasions were remodelled from an older brother's "blue broadcloth worn to fragility—so that Robert [the younger brother] said he could not look at them without making a rent;" and again the anticipation of the father's return from Philadelphia with gifts of necessaries and books.

After seventeen hundred and ninety-five Mr. Sedgwick was

compelled as a member of Congress to be away the greater part of each year, leaving household and farm to the care of an invalid wife. Memories of Mr. Sedgwick's infrequent visits home were mingled in his daughter's mind with the recollections of being kept up until nine o'clock to listen to his reading from Shakespeare, Don Quixote, or Hudibras. "Certainly," wrote Miss Sedgwick, "I did not understand them, but some glances of celestial light reached my soul, and I caught from his magnetic sympathy some elevation of feeling, and that love of reading which has been to me an 'education.'" "I was not more than twelve years old," she continues, "I think but ten—when one winter I read Rollin's Ancient History. The walking to our schoolhouse was often bad, and I took my lunch (how well I remember the bread and butter, and 'nut cake' and cold sausage, and nuts and apples that made the miscellaneous contents of that enchanting lunch-basket!), and in the interim between morning and afternoon school I crept under my desk (the desks were so made as to afford little close recesses under them) and read and munched and forgot myself in Cyrus' greatness."

It is beyond question that the keen relish induced by the scarcity of juvenile reading, together with the sound digestion it promoted, overbalanced in mental gain the novelties of a later day.

The Sedgwick library was probably typical of the average choice in reading-matter of the contemporary American child. Half a dozen little story-books, Berquin's "Children's Friend" (the very form and shade of color of its binding with its green edges were never forgotten by any member of the Sedgwick family), and the "Looking Glass for the Mind" were shelved side by side with a large volume entitled "Elegant Extracts," full of ballads, fables, and tales delightful to children whose imagination was already excited by the solemn mystery of Rowe's "Letters from the Dead to the Living." Since none of these books except those containing an infusion of religion were allowed to be read on Sunday, the Sedgwick children extended the bounds by turning over the pages of a book, and if the word "God" or "Lord" appeared, it was pounced upon as sanctified and therefore permissible.

Where families were too poor to buy story-books, the children found what amusement they could in the parents' small library. In ministers' families sermons were more plentiful than books. Mrs. H. B. Stowe, when a girl, found barrels of sermons in the garret of her father, the Rev. Dr. Beecher, in Litchfield, Connecticut. Through these sermons his daughter searched hungrily for mental food. It seemed as if there were thousands of the most unintelligible things. "An appeal on the unlawfulness of a man's marrying his wife's sister" turned up in every barrel by the dozens, until she despaired of finding an end of it. At last an ancient volume of "Arabian Nights" was unearthed. Here was the one inexhaustible source of delight to a child so eager for books that at ten years of age she had pored over the two volumes of the "Magnalia."

The library advantages of a more fortunately placed old-fashioned child we know from Dr. Holmes's frequent reference to incidents of his boyhood. He frankly confessed that he read in and not through many of the two thousand books in his father's library; but he found much to interest him in the volumes of periodicals, especially in the "Annual Register" and Rees's "Encyclopedia." Although apparently allowed to choose from the book-shelves, there were frequent evidences of a parent's careful supervision. "I remember," he once wrote to a friend, "many leaves were torn out of a copy of Dryden's Poems, with the comment 'Hiatus haud diflendus,' but I had like all children a kind of Indian sagacity in the discovery of contraband reading, such as a boy carries to a corner for perusal. Sermons I had enough from the pulpit. I don't know that I ever read one sermon of my own accord during my childhood. The 'Life of David,' by Samuel Chandler, had adventures enough, to say nothing of gallantry, in it to stimulate and gratify curiosity." "Biographies of Pious Children," wrote Dr. Holmes at another time, "were not to my taste. Those young persons were generally sickly, melancholy, and buzzed around by ghostly comforters or discomforters in a way that made me sick to contemplate." Again, Dr. Holmes, writing of the revolt from the commonly accepted religious doctrines he experienced upon reading the Rev. Thomas Scott's Family Bible, contrasted the gruesome doctrines it set forth with the story of Christian told in "Pilgrim's Progress," a book which captivated his imagination.

As to story-books, Dr. Holmes once referred to Mrs. Barbauld and Dr. Aikin's joint production, "Evenings at Home," with an accuracy bearing testimony to his early love for natural science. He also paid a graceful tribute to Lady Bountiful of "Little King Pippin" in comparing her in a conversation "At the Breakfast Table" with the appearance of three maiden ladies "rustling through the aisles of the old meeting-house, in silk and satin, not gay but more than decent."

Although Dr. Holmes was not sufficiently impressed with the contents of Miss Edgeworth's tales to mention them, at least one of her books contained much of the sort of information he found attractive in "Evenings at Home." "Harry and Lucy," besides pointing a moral on every page, foreshadowed that taste for natural science which turned every writer's thought toward printing geographical walks, botanical observations, natural history conversations, and geological dissertations in the guise of toy-books of amusement. A batch of books issued in America during the first two decades of the nineteenth century is illustrative of this new fashion. These books, belonging to the Labor-in-Play school, may best be described in their American editions.

One hundred years ago the American publishers of toy works were devoting their attention to the make-up rather than to the contents of their wares. The steady progress of the industrial arts enabled a greater number of printers to issue juvenile books, whose attractiveness was increased by better illustrations; and also with the improved facilities for printing and publishing, the issues of the various firms became more individual. At the beginning of the century the cheaper books entirely lost their charming gilt, flowery Dutch, and silver wrappers, as home products came into use. Size and illustrations also underwent a change.

In Philadelphia, Benjamin and Jacob Johnson, and later Johnson and Warner, issued both tiny books two inches square, and somewhat larger volumes containing illustrations

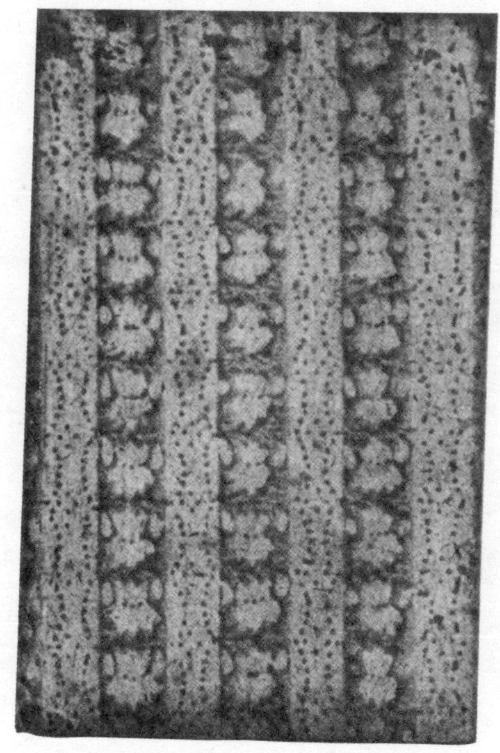

A Wall-paper Book-Cover

as well as text. These firms used for binding gray and blue marbled paper, gold-powdered yellow cardboard, or salmon pink, blue, and olive-green papers, usually without ornamentation. In eighteen hundred J. and J. Crukshank, of the same town, began to decorate with copper-plate cuts the outside of the white or blue paper covers of their imprints for children. Other printers followed their example, especially after wood-engraving became more generally used.

In Wilmington, Delaware, John Adams printed and sold "The New History of Blue Beard" in both peacock-blue and olive-green paper covers; but Peter Brynberg, also of that town, was still in eighteen hundred and four using quaint wall-paper to dress his toy imprints. Matthew Carey, the well-known printer of school-books for the children of Philadelphia, made a "Child's Guide to Spelling and Reading" more acceptable by a charming cover of yellow and red striped paper dotted over with little black hearts suggestive of the old Primer rhyme for the letter B:

> "My Book and Heart
> Shall never part."

In New York the dealers in juvenile books seem either to have bound in calf such classics as "The Blossoms of Morality," published by David Longworth at the Shakespeare Gallery in eighteen hundred and two, or in decorated but unattractive brown paper. This was the cover almost invariably used for years by Samuel Wood, the founder of the present publishing-house of medical works. He began in eighteen hundred and six to print the first of his many thousands of children's religious, instructive, and nursery books. As was the custom in order to insure a good sale, Wood first brought out a primer, "The Young Child's A B C." He decorated its Quaker gray cover with a woodcut of a flock of birds, and its title-page with a picture, presumably by Alexander Anderson, of a girl holding up a dove in her left hand and holding down a lamb with her right.

In New England, Nathaniel Coverly of Salem sometimes used a watered pink paper to cover his sixteen page toy-books, and in Boston his son, as late as eighteen hundred and thirteen, still used pieces of large patterned wall-paper for six-penny books, such as "Tom Thumb," "Old Mother Hubbard," and "Cock Robin."

The change in the appearance of most toy-books, however, was due largely to the increased use of illustrations. The work of the famous English engraver, Thomas Bewick, had at last been successfully copied by a physician of New York, Dr. Alexander Anderson.

Dr. Anderson was born in New York in seventeen hundred and seventy-five, and by seventeen hundred and ninety-three was employed by printers and publishers in New York, New Jersey, Philadelphia, and even Charleston to illustrate their books. Like other engravers, he began by cutting in type-metal, or engraving upon copper. In seventeen hundred and ninety-four, for Durell of New York, he undertook to make illustrations, probably for "The Looking Glass for the Mind." Beginning by copying Bewick's pictures upon type-metal, when "about one-third done, Dr. Anderson felt satisfied he could do better on wood."* In his diary we find noted

* Linton, *Wood Engraving in America.* Boston, 1882.

an instance of his perseverance in the midst of discouragement: "Sept. 24. This morning I was quite discouraged on seeing a crack in the wood. Employed as usual at the Doctor's, came home to dinner, glued the wood and began again with fresh hopes of producing a good wood engraving." September 26 found him "pretty well satisfied with the impression and so was Durell." In eighteen hundred he engraved all the pictures on wood for a new edition of the same book, and from this time he seems to have discontinued the use of type-metal, which he had employed in his earlier work as illustrator of the "Pilgrim's Progress" issued by Hugh Gaine, and of "Tom Thumb's Folio" printed by Brewer. After eighteen hundred and twelve Anderson almost gave up engraving on copper also, and devoted himself to satisfying the great demand for his work on wood. For Durell of New York, an extensive reprinter of English books, from toy-books to a folio edition of Josephus, he reproduced the English engravings, never making, according to Mr. Lossing, more than a frontispiece for the larger volumes.

Although Samuel Wood and Sons of New York also gave Dr. Anderson many orders for cuts for their various juvenile publications, he still found time to engrave for publishers of other cities. We find his illustrations in the toy-books printed in Boston and Philadelphia; and for Sidney Babcock, a New Haven publisher of juvenile literature, he supplied many of the numerous woodcuts required. The best of Anderson's work as an engraver coincided with the years of Babcock's very extensive business of issuing children's books, between 1805 and 1840. His cuts adorned the juvenile duodecimos that this printer's widely extended trade demanded; and even as far south as Charleston, South Carolina, Babcock, like Isaiah Thomas, found it profitable to open a branch shop.

Anderson's illustrations are the main features of most of Babcock's little blue, pink, and yellow paper-covered books; especially of those printed in the early years of the nineteenth century. We notice in them the changes in the dress of children, who no longer were clothed exactly in the semblance of their elders, but began to assume garments more appropriate to their ages, sports, and occupations. Anderson also sometimes introduced into his pictures a negro coachman or nurse in the place of the footman or maid of the English tale he illustrated.

While the demand for the engraver's work was constant, his remuneration was small, if we are to judge by Babcock's payment of only fifty shillings for fifteen cuts.

For these toy-books Anderson made many reproductions from Bewick's cuts, and although he did not equal the Englishman's work, he so far surpassed his pupils and imitators of the early part of the century that his engravings are generally to be recognized even when not signed. In eighteen hundred and two Dr. Anderson began to reproduce for David Longworth Bewick's "Quadrupeds," and these "cuts were afterwards made use of, with the Bewick letter-press also, for a series of children's books."*

In eighteen hundred and twelve, for Munroe & Francis of Boston, Dr. Anderson made after J. Thompson a set of cuts,

* Linton, *Wood Engraving in America.* Boston, 1882.

mainly remarkable "as the chief of his few departures from the style of his favorite, Bewick."*

The custom of not signing either text or engravings in the children's books has made it difficult to identify writers and illustrators of juvenile literature. But some of the best engravers undoubtedly practised their art on these toy-books. Nathaniel Dearborn, who was a stationer, printer, and engraver in Boston about eighteen hundred and eleven, sometimes signed the full-page illustrations on both wood and copper, and Abel Bowen, a copper-engraver, and possibly the first wood-engraver in Boston, signed a very curious publication entitled "A Metamorphosis"—a manifold paper which in its various possible combinations transformed one figure into another in keeping with the progress of the story.

C. Gilbert, a pupil of Mason, who had introduced the art of wood-engraving in Philadelphia from Boston, engraved on wood certainly the two full-page illustrations for "A Present for a Little Girl," printed in eighteen hundred and sixteen for a Baltimore firm, Warner & Hanna.

Adams and his pupils, Lansing and Morgan, also did work on children's books. Adams seems to have worked under Anderson's instruction, and after eighteen hundred and twenty-five did cuts for some books in the juvenile libraries of S. Wood and Mahlon Day of New York.

Of the engravers on copper, many tried their hands on these toy-books. Among them may be mentioned Amos Doolittle of New Haven, James Poupard, John Neagle, and W. Ralph of Philadelphia, and Rollinson of New York, who is credited

* Linton, *Wood Engraving in America.* Boston, 1882.

with having engraved the silver buttons on the coat worn by Washington on his inauguration as President.

But of the copper-plate engravers, perhaps none did more work for children's books than William Charles of Philadelphia. Charles, who is best known by his series of caricatures of the events of the War of 1812 and of local politics, worked upon toy-books as early as eighteen hundred and eight, when in Philadelphia he published in two parts "Tom the Piper's Son; illustrated with whimsical engravings." In these books both text and pictures were engraved, as will be seen in the illustration. Charles's plates for a series of moral tales in verse were used by his successors, Mary Charles, Morgan & Yeager, and Morgan & Sons, for certainly fifteen years after the originals were made. To William Charles the children in the vicinity of Philadelphia were also probably indebted for the introduction of colored pictures. It is possible that the young folks of Boston had the novelty of colored picture-books somewhat before Charles introduced them in Philadelphia, as we find that "The History and Adventures of Little Henry exemplified in a series of figures" was printed by J. Belcher of the Massachusetts town in 1812. These "figures" exhibited little Henry suitably attired for the various incidents of his career, with a movable head to be attached at will to any of the figures, which were not engraved with the text, but each was laid in loose on a blank page. William Charles's method of coloring the pictures engraved with the text was a slight advance, perhaps, upon the illustrations inserted separately; but it is doubtful whether these immovable plates afforded as much entertainment to little readers as the

The GOAT was a going to shave
off his beard,
But soon he was done when TOMS
music he heard,
He ran out of doors in a kind
of a passion,
And danced this fine dance
Which is now all the fashion.

Tom the Piper's Son

separate figures similar to paper dolls which Belcher, and somewhat later Charles also, used in a few of their publications.

The "Peacock at Home," engraved by Charles and then colored in aqua-tint, is one of the rare early colored picture-books still extant, having been first issued in eighteen hundred and fourteen. The coloring of the illustrations at first doubled the price, and seems to have been used principally for a series of stories belonging to what may be styled the Ethics-in-Play type of juvenile literature, and entitled the "History and Adventures of Little William," "Little Nancy," etc. These tales, written after the objective manner of Miss Edgeworth, glossed over by rhyme, contained usually eight colored plates, and sold for twenty-five cents each instead of twelve cents, the price of the picture-book without colored plates. Sometimes, as in the case of "Cinderella," we find the text illustrated with a number of "Elegant Figures, to dress and undress." The paper doll could be placed behind the costumes appropriate to the various adventures, and, to prevent the loss of the heroine, the book was tied up with pink or blue ribbon after the manner of a portfolio.

With engravers on wood and copper able to make more attractive the passion for instruction which marked the first quarter of the nineteenth century, the variety of toy-book literature naturally became greater. Indeed, without pictures to render somewhat entertaining the Labor-in-Play school, it is doubtful whether it could have attained its widespread popularity.

It is, of course, possible to name but a few titles typical of the various kinds of instruction offered as amusement. "To present to the young Reader a Little Miscellany of Natural History, Moral Precept, Sentiment, and Narrative," Dr. Kendall wrote "Keeper's Travels in Search of his Master," "The Canary Bird," and "The Sparrow." "The Prize for Youthful Obedience" endeavored to instill a love for animals, and to promote obedient habits. Its story runs in this way:

"A kind and good father had a little lively son, named Francis; but, although that little boy was six years old, he had not yet learned to read.

"His mama said to him, one day, 'if Francis will learn to read well, he shall have a pretty little chaise.'

"The little boy was vastly pleased with this; he presently spelt five or six words and then kissed his mama.

"'Mama,' said Francis, 'I am delighted with the thoughts of this chaise, but I should like to have a horse to draw it.'

"'Francis shall have a little dog, which will do instead of a horse,' replied his mama, 'but he must take care to give him some victuals, and not do him any harm.'"

The dog was purchased, and named Chloe. "She was as brisk as a bee, prettily spotted, and as gentle as a lamb." We are now prepared for trouble, for the lesson of the story is surely not hidden. Chloe was fastened to the chaise, a cat secured to serve as a passenger, and "Francis drove his little chaise along the walk." But "when he had been long enough among the gooseberry trees, his mama took him in the garden and told him the names of the flowers." We are thus led to suppose that Francis had never been in the garden before! The mother is called away. We feel sure that the trouble

A Kind and Good Father

anticipated is at hand. "As soon as she was gone Francis began whipping the dog," and of course when the dog dashed forward the cat tumbled out, and "poor Chloe was terrified by the chaise which banged on all sides. Francis now heartily repented of his cruel behaviour and went into the house crying, and looking like a very simple boy."

"I see very plainly the cause of this misfortune," said the father, who, however, soon forgave his repentant son. Thereafter every day Francis learned his lesson, and was rewarded by facts and pictures about animals, by table-talks, or by walks about the country.

Knowledge offered within small compass seems to have been a novelty introduced in Philadelphia by Jacob Johnson, who had a juvenile library in High Street.

In eighteen hundred and three he printed two tiny volumes entitled "A Description of Various Objects." Bound in green paper covers, the two-inch square pages were printed in bold type. The first volume contained the illustrations of the objects described in the other. The characterizations were exceedingly short, as, for example, this of the "Puppet Show:" "Here are several little boys and girls looking at a puppet show, I suppose you would like to make one of them."

Four years later Johnson improved upon this, when he printed in better type "People of all Nations; an useful toy for Girl or Boy." Of approximately the same size as the other volumes, it was bound with stiff sides and calf back. The plates, engraved on copper, represent men of various nationalities in the favorite alphabetical order. A is an American. V is a Virginian,—an Indian in scant costume of feathers with a long pipe, — who, the printed description says, "is generally dressed after the manner of the English; but this is a poor African, and made a slave of." An orang-outang represents the letter O, and according to the author, is "a wild man of the woods, in the East Indies. He sleeps under trees, and builds himself a hut. He cannot speak, but when the natives make a fire in the woods he will come and warm himself." Ten years later there was still some difficulty in getting exact descriptions of unfamiliar animals. Thus in "A Familiar Description of Beasts and Birds" the baboon is drawn with a dog's body and an uncanny head with a snout. The reader is informed that "the baboon has a long face resembling a dog's; his eyes are red and very bright, his teeth are large and strong, but his swiftness renders him hard to be taken. He delights in fishing, and will stay for a considerable time under water. He imitates several of our actions, and will drink wine, and eat human food."

Another series of three books, written by William Darton, the English publisher and maker of toy-books, was called "Chapters of Accidents, containing Caution and Instruction." Thrilling accounts of "Escapes from Danger" when robbing birds'-nests and hunting lions and tigers were intermingled with wise counsel and lessons to be gained from an "Upset Cart," or a "Balloon Excursion." With one incident the Philadelphia printer took the liberty of changing the title to "Cautions to Walkers on the Streets of Philadelphia." High Street, now Market Street, is represented in a picture of the young woman who, unmindful of the warning, "Never to turn hastily around the corner of a street," "ran against the

a Virginian

A Baboon

porter's load and nearly lost one of her eyes." The change, of course, is worthy of notice only because of the slight effort to locate the story in America.

An attempt to familiarize children with flowers resulted in two tales, called "The Rose's Breakfast" and "Flora's Gala," in which flowers were personified as they took part in fêtes. "Garden Amusements, for Improving the Minds of Little Children," was issued by Samuel Wood of New York with this advertisement: "This little treatise, (written and first published in the great emporium of the British nation) containing so many pleasing remarks for the juvenile mind, was thought worthy of an American edition. . . . Being so very natural, . . . and its tendency so moral and amusing, it is to be hoped an advantage will be obtained from its re-publication in Freedonia."

Dialogue was the usual method of instruction employed by Miss Edgeworth and her followers. In "Garden Amusements" the conversation was interrupted by a note criticising a quotation from Milton as savoring too much of poetic license. Cowper also gained the anonymous critic's disapproval, although it was his point of view and not his style that came under censure.

In still another series of stories often reprinted from London editions were those moral tales with the sub-title "Cautionary Stories in Verse." Mr. William James used these "Cautionary Verses for Children" as an example of the manner in which "the muse of evangelical protestantism in England, with the mind fixed on the ideas of danger, had at last drifted away from the original gospel of freedom." "Chronic anxiety,"

Mr. James continued, "marked the earlier part of this [nineteenth] century in evangelical circles." A little salmon-colored volume, "The Daisy," is a good example of this series. Each rhyme is a warning or an admonition; a chronic fear that a child might be naughty. "Drest or Undrest" is typical of the sixteen hints for the proper conduct of every-day life contained in the innocent "Daisy:"

"When children are naughty and will not be drest,
Pray what do you think is the way?
Why, often I really believe it is best
To keep them in night-clothes all day!

"But then they can have no good breakfast to eat,
Nor walk with their mother and aunt;
At dinner they'll have neither pudding nor meat,
Nor anything else that they want.

"Then who would be naughty and sit all the day
In night-clothes unfit to be seen!
And pray who would lose all their pudding and play
For not being drest neat and clean."

Two other sets of books with a like purpose were brought out by Charles about eighteen hundred and sixteen. One began with those familiar nursery verses entitled "My Mother," by Ann Taylor, which were soon followed by "My Father," all the family, "My Governess," and even "My Pony." The other set of books was "calculated to promote Benevolence and Virtue in Children." "Little Fanny," "Little Nancy," and "Little Sophie" were all held up as warnings of the results of pride, greed, and disobedience.

The difference between these heroines of fiction and the characters drawn by Maria Edgeworth lies mainly in the fact

Drest or Undrest

that they spoke in rhyme instead of in prose, and that they were almost invariably naughty; or else the parents were cruel and the children suffered. Rarely do we find a cheerful tale such as "The Cherry Orchard" in this cautionary style of toy-book. Still more rarely do we find any suspicion of that alloy of nonsense supposed by Miss Edgeworth to make the sense work well. It is all quite serious. "Little Nancy, or, the Punishment of Greediness," is representative of this sort of moral and cautionary tale. The frontispiece, "embellishing" the first scene, shows Nancy in receipt of an invitation to a garden party:

"Now the day soon appear'd
But she very much fear'd
She should not be permitted to go.
Her best frock she had torn,
The last time it was worn;
Which was very vexatious, you know."

However, the mother consents with the *caution:*

"Not to greedily eat
The nice things at the treat;
As she much wished to break her of this."

Arrived at the party, Nancy shared the games, and

"At length was seated,
With her friends to be treated;
So determin'd on having her share,
That she drank and she eat
Ev'ry thing she could get,
Yet still she was loth to forbear."

The disastrous consequences attending Nancy's disregard of her mother's admonition are displayed in a full-page illustration, which is followed by another depicting the sorrowful end in bed of the day's pleasure. Then the moral:

"My young readers beware,
And avoid with great care
Such *excesses* as these you 've just read;
For be sure you will find
It your interest to mind
What your friends and relations have said."

Perhaps of all the toy imprints of the early century none are more curious in modern eyes than the three or four German translations printed by Philadelphia firms. In eighteen hundred and nine Johnson and Warner issued "Kleine Erzählungen über ein Buch mit Kupfern." This seems to be a translation of "A Mother's Remarks over a Set of Cuts," and contains a reference to another book entitled "Anecdoten von Hunden." Still another book is extant, printed in eighteen hundred and five by Zentler, "Unterhaltungen für Deutsche Kinder." This, according to its preface, was one of a series for which Jacob and Benjamin Johnson had consented to lend the plates for illustrations.

Patriotism, rather than diversion, still characterized the very little original work of the first quarter of the century for American children. A book with the imposing title of "Geographical, Statistical and Political Amusement" was published in Philadelphia in eighteen hundred and six. "This work," says its advertisement, "is designed as an easy means of uniting Instruction with Pleasure . . . to entice the youthful mind to an acquaintance with a species of information [about the United States] highly useful."

"The Juvenile Magazine, or Miscellaneous Repository of Useful Information," issued in eighteen hundred and three, contained as its only original contribution an article upon General Washington's will, "an affecting and most original composition," wrote the editor. This was followed seven years later by the well-known "Life of George Washington," by M. L. Weems, in which was printed the now famous and disputed cherry-tree incident. Its abridged form known to present day nursery lore differs from the long drawn out account by Weems, who, like Thomas Day, risked being diffuse in his desire to show plainly his moral. The last part of the story sufficiently gives his manner of writing:

"Presently George and his hatchet made their appearance. 'George,' said his father, 'do you know who killed that beautiful little cherry tree yonder in the garden?' That was a tough question; and George staggered under it for a moment; but quickly recovered himself, and looking at his father, with the sweet face of youth brightened with the inexpressible charm of all conquering truth, he bravely cried out, 'I can't tell a lie, Pa; you know I can't tell a lie. I did cut it with my hatchet!' 'Run to my arms, you dearest boy,' cried his father in transports, 'run to my arms; glad am I, George, that you killed my tree; for you have paid me for it a thousand fold. Such an act of heroism is worth more than a thousand trees, though blossomed with silver, and their fruits of purest gold.'"

Franklin's "Way to Wealth" was considered to be perfectly adapted to all children's comprehension, and was issued by various publishers of juvenile books. By eighteen hundred and eight it was illustrated and sold "with fine engravings for twenty-five cents."

Of patriotic poetry there was much for grown folks, but the "Patriotic and Amatory Songster," advertised by S. Avery of Boston about the time Weems's biography was published, seems a title ill-suited to the juvenile public for whom Avery professed to issue it.

Among the books which may be cited as furnishing instructive amusement with less of the admixture of moral purpose was the "London Cries for Children," with pictures of street peddlers. This was imitated in America by the publication of the "Cries of New York" and "Cries of Philadelphia."

In the Lenox Collection there is now one of the various editions of the "Cries of New York" (published in 1808), which is valuable both as a record of the street life of the old-fashioned town of ninety-six thousand inhabitants, and as perhaps the first child's book of purely local interest, with original woodcuts very possibly designed and engraved by Alexander Anderson.

The "Cries of New York" is of course modelled after the "London Cries," but the account it gives of various incidents in the daily life of old New York makes us grateful for the existence of this child's toy. A picture of a chimney-sweep, for instance, is copied, with his cry of "Sweep, O, O, O, O," from the London book, but the text accompanying it is altered to accord with the custom in New York of firing a gun at dawn:

"About break of day, after the morning gun is heard from

Governor's Island, and so through the forenoon, the ears of the citizens are greeted with this uncouth sound from figures as unpleasant to the sight, clothed in rags and covered with soot—a necessary and suffering class of human beings indeed—spending their childhood thus. And in regard to the unnecessary bawling of those sooty boys; it is *admirable* in such a noisy place as this, where every needless sound should be hushed, that such disagreeable ones should be allowed. The prices for sweeping chimneys are—one story houses twelve cents; two stories, eighteen cents; three stories, twenty-five cents, and so on."

"Hot Corn" was also cried by children, whose business it was to "gather cents, by distributing corn to those who are disposed to regale themselves with an ear." Baked pears are pictured as sold "by a little black girl, with the pears in an earthen dish under her arm." At the same season of the year, "Here's your fine ripe water-melons" also made itself heard above the street noises as a street cry of entirely American origin. Again there were pictured "Oyster Stands," served by negroes, and these were followed by cries of

> "Fine Clams: choice Clams,
> Here's your Rock-a-way beach
> Clams: here's your fine
> Young, sand Clams,"

from Flushing Cove Bay, which the text explains, "turn out as good, or perhaps better," than oysters. The introduction of negroes and negro children into the illustrations is altogether a novelty, and together with the scenes drawn from the street life of the town gave to the old-fashioned child its first distinctly American picture-book. Indeed, with the exception of this and an occasional illustration in some otherwise English reproduction, all the American publishers at this time seem to have modelled their wares for small children after those of two large London firms, J. Harris, successor to Newbery, and William Darton.

To Darton, the author of "Little Truths," the children were indebted for a serious attempt to improve the character of toy-books. A copper-plate engraver by profession, Darton's attention was drawn to the scarcity of books for children by the discovery that there was not much written for them that was worth illustrating. Like Newbery, he set about to make books himself, and with John Harvey, also an engraver, he set up in Grace Church Street an establishment for printing and publishing, from which he supplied, to a great extent, the juvenile books closely imitated by American printers. Besides his own compositions, he was very alert to encourage promising authors, and through him the famous verses of Jane and Ann Taylor were brought into notice. "Original Poems," and "Rhymes for the Nursery," by these sisters, were to the old-time child what Stevenson's "Child's Garden of Verses" is to the modern nursery. Darton and Harvey paid ten pounds for the first series of "Original Poems," and fifteen pounds for the second; while "Rhymes for the Nursery" brought to its authors the unusual sum of twenty pounds. The Taylors were the originators of that long series of verses for infants which "My Sister" and "My Governess" strove to surpass but never in any way equalled, although they apparently met with a fair sale in America.

Little Nancy

Enterprising American booksellers also copied the new ways of advertising juvenile books. An instance of this is afforded by Johnson and Warner of Philadelphia, who apparently succeeded Jacob and Benjamin Johnson, and had, by eighteen hundred and ten, branch shops in Richmond, Virginia, and Lexington, Kentucky. They advertised their "neatly executed books of amusement" in book notes in the "Young Gentlemen and Ladies' Magazine," by means of digressions from the thread of their stories, and sometimes by inserting as frontispiece a rhyme taken from one used by John Harris of St. Paul's Churchyard:

"At JO— store in Market Street
A sure reward good children meet.
In coming home the other day
I heard a little master say
For ev'ry three-pence there he took
He had received a little book.
With covers neat and cuts so pretty
There's not its like in all the city;
And that for three-pence he could buy
A story book would make one cry;
For little more a book of Riddles:
Then let us not buy drums and fiddles
Nor yet be stopped at pastry cooks',
But spend our money all in books;
For when we've learnt each bit by heart
Mamma will treat us with a tart."

Later, when engraving had become more general in use, William Charles cut for an advertisement, as frontispiece to some of his imprints, an interior scene containing a shelf of books labelled "W. Charles' Library for Little Folks." About the same time another form of advertisement came into use. This was the publisher's *Recommendation*, which frequently accompanied the narrative in place of a preface. The "Story of Little Henry and his Bearer," by Mrs. Sherwood, a writer of many English Sunday-school tales, contained the announcement that it was "fraught with much useful instruction. It is recommended as an excellent thing to be put in the hands of children; and grown persons will find themselves well paid for the trouble of reading it."

Little Henry belonged to the Sunday-school type of hero, one whose biography Dr. Holmes doubtless avoided when possible. Yet no history of toy-books printed presumably for children's amusement as well as instruction should omit this favorite story, which represents all others of its class of Religion-in-Play books. The following incidents are taken from an edition printed by Lincoln and Edmunds of Boston. This firm made a special feature of "Books suitable for Presents in Sunday-School." They sold wholesale for eight dollars a hundred, such tales as Taylor's "Hymns for Infant Minds," "Friendly Instruction," Fenelon's "Reflections," Doddridge's "Principles of the Christian Religion," "Pleasures of Piety in Youth," "Walks of Usefulness," "Practical Piety," etc.

The objective point of little Henry's melancholy history was to prove the "Usefulness of Female Missionaries," said its editor, Mrs. Cameron, a sister of the author, who at the time was herself living in India. Mrs. Sherwood based the thread of her story upon the life of a household in India, but it winds itself mainly around the conversion of the faithful Indian bearer who served five-year-old Henry. This small orphan was one of those morbidly religious children who "never said a bad word and was vexed when he heard any other person do it." He also, although himself "saved by grace," as the phrase then ran in evangelical circles, was chronically anxious lest he should offend the Lord. To quote verbatim from this relic of the former religious life would savor too much of ridiculing those things that were sacred and serious to the people of that day. Yet the main incidents of the story were these: Henry's conversion took place after a year and a half of hard work on the part of a missionary, who finally had the satisfaction of bringing little Henry "from the state of grossest heathen darkness and ignorance to a competent knowledge of those doctrines necessary to salvation." This was followed immediately by the offer of Henry to give all his toys for a Bible with a purple morocco cover. Then came the preparations for the teacher's departure, when she called him to her room and catechized him in a manner worthy of Cotton Mather a century before. After his teacher's departure the boy, mindful of the lady's final admonition, sought to make a Christian of his bearer, Boosy. Like so many story-book parents, Henry's mother was altogether neglectful of her child; and consequently he was left much to the care of Boosy—time which he improved with "arguments with Boosy concerning the great Creator of things." But it is not necessary to follow Henry through his ardent missionary efforts to the admission of the black boy of his sinful state, nor to the time when the hero was delivered from this evil world. Enough has been said to show that the religious child of fiction was not very different from little

Elizabeth Butcher or Hannah Hill of colonial days, whose pious sayings were still read when "Little Henry" was introduced to the American child.

Indeed, when Mrs. Sherwood's fictitious children were not sufficiently religious to come up to the standard of five-year-old Henry, their parents were invariably as pious as the father of the "Fairchild Family." This was imported and reprinted for more than one generation as a "best seller." It was almost a modernized version of Janeway's "Token for Children," with Mather's supplement of "A Token for the Children of New England," in its frequent production of death-bed scenes, together with painful object lessons upon the sinfulness of every heart. To impress such lessons Mr. Fairchild spared his family no sight of horror or distress. He even took them to see a man on the gallows, "that," said the ingenuous gentleman, "they may love each other with a perfect and heavenly love." As the children gazed upon the dreadful object the tender father described in detail its every phase, and ended by kneeling in prayer. The story of Evelyn in the third chapter was written as the result of a present of books from an American *Universalist*, whose doctrines Mrs. Sherwood thought likely to be pernicious to children and should be controverted as soon as possible. Later, other things emanating from America were considered injurious to children, but this seems to be the first indication that American ideas were noticed in English juvenile literature.

But all this lady's tales were not so lugubrious, and many were immense favorites. Children were even named for the hero of the "Little Millenium Boy." Publishers frequently sent her orders for books to be "written to cuts," and the "Busy Bee," the "Errand Boy," and the "Rose" were some of the results of this method of supplying the demand for her work. Naturally, Mrs. Sherwood, like Miss Edgeworth, had many imitators, but if we could believe the incidents related as true to life, parents would seem to have been either very indifferent to their children or forever suspicious of them. In Newbery's time it had been thought no sin to wear fine buckled shoes, to be genteelly dressed with a wide "ribband;" but now the vain child was one who wore a white frock with pink sash, towards whom the finger of scorn was pointed, and from whom the moral was unfailingly drawn. Vanity was, apparently, an unpardonable sin, as when in a "Moral Tale,"

> "Mamma observed the rising lass
> By stealth retiring to the glass
> To practise little arts unseen
> In the true genius of thirteen."

The constant effort to draw a lesson from every action sometimes led to overstepping the bounds of truth by the parents themselves, as for example in a similar instance of love for a mirror. "What is this I see, Harriet?" asked a mother in "Emulation." "Is that the way you employ your precious time? I am no longer surprised at the alteration in your looks of late, that you have appeared so sickly, have lost your complexion; in short I have twenty times been on the point of asking you if you are ill. You look shockingly, child."

"I am very well, Mamma, indeed," cried Harriet, quite alarmed.

"Impossible, my dear, you can never look well, while you

follow such an unwholesome practice. Looking-glasses were never intended for little girls, and very few sensible people use them as there is something really poisonous in their composition. To use them is not only prejudicial to the health but to the disposition."

Although this conception of the use of looking-glasses as prejudicial to right living seems to hark back to the views expressed in the old story of the "Prodigal Daughter," who sat before a mirror when the Devil made his second appearance, yet the world of story-book literature, even though its creators were sometimes either careless or ignorant of facts, now also emphasized the value of general knowledge, which it endeavored to pour in increasing quantity into the nursery. Miss More had started the stream of goody-goody books, while Miss Edgeworth, Mrs. Barbauld, and Thomas Day were the originators of the deluge of conversational bores, babies, boys, and teachers that threatened to flood the family bookshelves of America when the American writers for children came upon the scene.

CHAPTER VII

1825–1840

Old story-books! old story-books! we owe you much, old friends,
Bright-coloured threads in Memory's warp, of which Death holds the ends.
Who can forget? Who can spurn the ministers of joy
That waited on the lisping girl and petticoated boy?
Talk of your vellum, gold embossed, morocco, roan, and calf;
The blue and yellow wraps of old were prettier by half.

Eliza Cooke

Their works of amusement, when not laden with more religion than the tale can hold in solution, are often admirable.

Quarterly Review, 1843

CHAPTER VII

1825–1840

American Writers and English Critics

IT is customary to refer to the early writings of Washington Irving as works that marked the time when literature pure and simple developed in America. Such writing as had hitherto attracted attention concerned itself, not with matters of the imagination, but with facts and theories of current and momentous interest. Religion and the affairs of the separate commonwealths were uppermost in people's minds in colonial days; political warfare and the defence of the policy of Congress absorbed attention in Revolutionary times; and later the necessity of expounding principles of government and of fostering a national feeling produced a literature of fact rather than of fancy.

Gradually all this had changed. A new generation had grown up with more leisure for writing and more time to devote to the general culture of the public. The English periodical with its purpose of "improving the taste, awakening the attention, and amending the heart," had once met these requirements. Later on these periodicals had been keenly enjoyed, but at the same time there appeared American magazines, modelled after them, but largely filled by contributions from literary Americans. Early in the nineteenth century such publications were current in most large towns. From the short essays and papers in these periodicals to the tales of Cooper and Irving the step, after all, was not a long one.

The children's literature of amusement developed, after the

end of the eighteenth century, in a somewhat similar way, although as usual tagging along after that of their parents.

With the constantly increasing population the production of children's books grew more profitable, and in eighteen hundred and two Benjamin Johnson made an attempt to publish a "Juvenile Magazine" in Philadelphia. Its purpose was to be a "Miscellaneous Repository of Useful Information;" but the contents were so largely drawn from English sources that it was probably, like the toy-books, pirated from an English publisher. Indeed, one of the few extant volumes contains only one article of distinctly American composition among essays on *Education*, the *Choice of a Wife*, *Love*, papers on natural history, selections from poems by Coleridge and Cowper; and by anonymous makers of verse about *Consumption* and *Friendship*. The American contribution, a discussion of President Washington's will, has already been mentioned.

In the same year, 1802, the "Juvenile Olio" was started, edited by "Amyntor," but like Johnson's "Juvenile Magazine," was only issued at irregular intervals and was short-lived.

Other ventures in children's periodicals continued to be made, however. The "Juvenile Magazine," with "Religious, Moral, and Entertaining Pieces in Prose and Verse," was compiled by Arthur Donaldson, and sold in eighteen hundred and eleven as a monthly in Philadelphia—then the literary centre—for twelve and a half cents a number. In eighteen hundred and thirteen, in the same city, the "Juvenile Portfolio" made its appearance, possibly in imitation of Joseph Dennie's "Port Folio;" but it too failed from lack of support and interest.

Boston proved more successful in arousing attention to the possibilities in a well-conducted children's periodical, although it was not until thirteen years later that Lydia Maria Child established the "Juvenile Miscellany for the Instruction and Amusement of Youth." Three numbers were issued in 1826, and thereafter it appeared every other month until August, 1834, when it was succeeded by a magazine of the same name conducted by Sarah J. Hale.

This periodical is a landmark in the history of story-writing for the American child. Here at last was an opportunity for the editors to give to their subscribers descriptions of cities in their own land in place of accounts of palaces in Persia; biographies of national heroes instead of incidents in the life of Mahomet; and tales of Indians rather than histories of Arabians and Turks. For its pages Mrs. Sigourney, Miss Eliza Leslie, Mrs. Wells, Miss Sedgwick, and numerous anonymous contributors gladly sent stories of American scenes and incidents which were welcomed by parents as well as by children.

In the year following the first appearance of Mrs. Hale's "Juvenile Miscellany," the March number is typical of the amusement and instruction the editor endeavored to provide. This contained a life of Benjamin Franklin (perhaps the earliest child's life of the philosopher and statesman), a tale of an Indian massacre of an entire settlement in Maine, an essay on memory, a religious episode, and extracts from a traveller's journal. The traveller, quite evidently a Bostonian, criticised New York in a way not unfamiliar in later days, as a city where "the love of literature was less strong than in some other parts of the United States;" and then in trying to soften the statement, she fell into a comparison with Philadelphia, also made many times since the gentle critic observed the difference. "New York," she wrote, "has energy, spirit, and bold, lofty enterprise, totally wanting in Philadelphia, . . . a place of neat, well regulated plans." Also, like the English story-book of the previous century, this American "Miscellany" introduced *Maxims for a Student*, found, it cheerfully explained, "among the manuscripts of a deceased friend." Puzzles and conundrums made an entertaining feature, and as the literary *chef d'œuvre* was inserted a poem supposed to be composed by a babe in South Carolina, but of which the author was undoubtedly Mrs. Gilman, whose ideas of a baby's ability were certainly not drawn from her own nursery.

A rival to the "Juvenile Miscellany" was the "Youth's Companion," established at this time in Boston by Nathaniel P. Willis and the Reverend Asa Rand. The various religious societies also began to issue children's magazines for Sunday perusal: the Massachusetts Sunday School Union beginning in 1828 the "Sabbath School Times," and other societies soon following its example.

"Parley's Magazine," planned by Samuel G. Goodrich and published by Lilly, Wait and Company of Boston, ran a successful course of nine years from eighteen hundred and thirty-three. The prospectus declared the intention of its conductors "to give descriptions of manners, customs, and countries, Travels, Voyages, and Adventures in Various parts of the world, interesting historical notes, Biography, particularly of young persons, original tales, cheerful and pleasing Rhymes, and to issue the magazine every fortnight." The popularity of the name of Peter Parley insured a goodly number of subscriptions from the beginning, and the life of "Parley's Magazine" was somewhat longer than any of its predecessors.

In the south the idea of issuing a juvenile magazine was taken up by a firm in Charleston, and the "Rose Bud" was started in eighteen hundred and thirty. The "Rose Bud," a weekly, was largely the result of the success of the "Juvenile Miscellany," as the editor of the southern paper, Mrs. Gilman, was a valued contributor to the "Miscellany," and had been encouraged in her plan of a paper for children of the south by the Boston conductors of the northern periodical.

Mrs. Gilman was born in Boston, and at sixteen years of age had published a poem most favorably criticised at the time. Marrying a clergyman who settled in Charleston, she continued her literary work, but was best known to our grandmothers as the author of "Recollections of a New England Housekeeper." The "Rose Bud" soon blossomed into the "Southern Rose," a family paper, but faded away in 1839.

Among other juvenile weeklies of the time may be mentioned the "Juvenile Rambler" and the "Hive," which are chiefly interesting by reason of the opportunity their columns offered to youthful contributors.

Another series of "miscellaneous repositories" for the instructive enjoyment of little people was furnished by the Annuals of the period. These, of course, were modelled after the adult Annuals revolving in social circles and adorning the marble-topped tables of drawing-rooms in both England and America.

Issued at the Christmas and New Year seasons, these children's Annuals formed the conventional gift-book for many years, and publishers spared no effort to make them attractive. Indeed, their red morocco, silk, or embossed scarlet cloth bindings form a cheerful contrast to the dreary array of black and drab cloth covering the fiction of both old and young. Better illustrations were also introduced than the ugly cuts "adorning" the other books for juvenile readers. Oliver Pelton, Joseph Andrews (who ranked well as an engraver), Elisha Gallaudet, Joseph G. Kellogg, Joseph I. Pease, and Thomas Illman were among the workers in line-engraving whose early work served to illustrate, often delightfully, these popular collections of children's stories.

Among the "Annualettes," "Keepsakes," "Evening Hours," and "Infant's Hours" published at intervals after eighteen hundred and twenty-five the "Token" stands preëminent. Edited by Samuel G. Goodrich (Peter Parley) between the years eighteen hundred and twenty-eight and eighteen hundred and forty-two, its contents and illustrations were almost entirely American. Edward Everett, Bishop Doane, A. H. Everett, John Quincy Adams, Longfellow, Hawthorne, Miss Sedgwick, Eliza Leslie, Dr. Holmes, Horace Greeley, James T. Fields, and Gulian Verplanck—all were called upon to make the "Token" an annual treat to children. Of the many stories written for it, only Hawthorne's "Twice Told Tales" survive; but the long list of contributors of mark in American literature cannot be surpassed to-day by any child's book by contemporary authors. The contents, although written in the style of eighty years ago, are undoubtedly good from a literary standpoint, however out of date their story-telling quali-

Children of the Cottage

ties may be. And, moreover, the "Token" assuredly gave pleasure to the public for which its yearly publication was made.

By eighteen hundred and thirty-five the "Annual" was in full swing as a popular publication. Then an international book was issued, "The American Juvenile Keepsake," edited by Mrs. Hofland, the well-known writer of English stories for children. Mrs. Hofland cried up her wares in a manner quite different from that of the earlier literary ladies. "My table of contents," she wrote in her introduction, "exhibits a list of names not exceeded in reputation by any preceding Juvenile Annual; for, although got up with a celerity almost distressing in the hurry it imposed, such has been the kindness of my literary friends, that they have left me little more to wish for." Among the English contributors were Miss Mitford, Miss Jean Roberts, Miss Browne, and Mrs. Hall, the ablest writers for English children, and already familiar to American households.

Mrs. Hofland, herself, wrote one of its stories, noteworthy as an early attempt of an English author to write for an American juvenile public. She found her theme in the movement of emigration strong in England just then among the laboring people. No amount of discouragement and bitter criticism of the United States by the British press was sufficient to stem appreciably the tide of laborers that flowed towards the country whence came information of better wages and more work. Mrs. Hofland, although writing for little Americans, could not wholly resist the customary fling at American life and society. She acknowledged, however, that long residence altered first impressions and brought out the kernel of American character, whose husk only was visible to sojourners. She deplored the fact that "gay English girls used only to the polished society of London were likely to return with the impression that the men were rude and women frivolous." This impression the author was inclined to believe unjust, yet deemed it wise, because of the incredulous (perhaps even in America!), to back her own opinion by a note saying that this view was also shared by a valued friend who had lived fourteen years in Raleigh, South Carolina.

Having thus done justice, in her own eyes, to conditions in the new country, Mrs. Hofland, launched the laborer's family upon the sea, and followed their travels from New York to Lexington, Kentucky, at that time a land unknown to the average American child beyond some hazy association with the name of Daniel Boone. It was thus comparatively safe ground on which to place the struggles of the immigrants, who prospered because of their English thrift and were an example to the former residents. Of course the son grew up to prove a blessing to the community, and eventually, like the heroes in old Isaiah Thomas's adaptations of Newbery's good boys, was chosen Congressman.

There is another point of interest in connection with this English author's tale. Whether consciously or not, it is a very good imitation of Peter Parley's method of travelling with his characters in various lands or over new country. It is, perhaps, the first instance in the history of children's literature of an American story-writer influencing the English writer of juvenile fiction. And it was not the only time. So popular and profitable did Goodrich's style of story become that somewhat later the frequent attempts to exploit anonymously and profitably his pseudonymn in England as well as in America were loudly lamented by the originator of the "Tales of Peter Parley." It is, moreover, suggestive of the gradual change in the relations between the two countries that anything written in America was thought worth imitating. America, indeed, was beginning to supply incidents around which to weave stories for British children and tales altogether made at home for her own little readers.

In the same volume Mrs. S. C. Hall also boldly attempted to place her heroine in American surroundings. Philadelphia was the scene chosen for her tale; but, having flattered her readers by this concession to their sympathies and interest, the author was still sufficiently insular to doubt the existence of a competent local physician in this the earliest medical centre in the United States. An English family had come to make their home in the city, where the mother's illness necessitated the attendance of a French doctor to make a correct diagnosis of her case. An operation was advised, which the mother, Mrs. Allen, hesitated to undergo in an unknown land. Emily, the fourteen-year-old daughter, urged her not to delay, as she felt quite competent to be in attendance, having had "five teeth drawn without screaming; nursed a brother through the whooping-cough and a sister through the measles."

"Ma foi, Mademoiselle," said the French doctor, "you are very heroic; why, let me see, you talk of being present at an operation, which I would not hardly suffer my junior pupils to attend."

"Put," said the heroic damsel, "my resolution, sir, to any test you please; draw one, two, three teeth, I will not flinch." And this courage the writer thought could not be surpassed in a London child. It is needless to say that Emily's fortitude was sufficient to endure the sight of her mother's suffering, and to nurse her to complete recovery. Evidently residence in America had not yet sapped the young girl's moral strength, or reduced her to the frivolous creature an American woman was reputed in England to be.

Among the home contributors to "The American Juvenile Keepsake" were William L. Stone, who wrote a prosy article about animals; and Mrs. Embury, called the Mitford of America (because of her stories of village life), who furnished a religious tale to controvert the infidel doctrines considered at the time subtly undermining to childish faith, with probable reference to the Unitarian movement then gaining many adherents. Mrs. Embury's stories were so generally gloomy, being strongly tinged with the melancholy religious views of certain church denominations, that one would suppose them to have been eminently successful in turning children away from the faith she sought to encourage. For this "Keepsake" the same lady let her poetical fancy take flight in "The Remembrance of Youth is a Sigh," a somewhat lugubrious and pessimistic subject for a child's Christmas Annual. Occasionally a more cheerful mood possessed "Ianthe," as she chose to call herself, and then we have some of the earliest descriptions of country life in literature for American children. There is one especially charming picture of a walk in New England woods upon a crisp October day, when the children merrily

Henrietta

hunt for chestnuts among the dry brown leaves, and the squirrels play above their heads in the many colored boughs.

Dr. Holmes has somewhere remarked upon the total lack of American nature descriptions in the literature of his boyhood. No birds familiar to him were ever mentioned; nor were the flowers such as a New England child could ever gather. Only English larks and linnets, cowslips and hawthorn, were to be found in the toy-books and little histories read to him. "Everything was British: even the robin, a domestic bird," wrote the doctor, "instead of a great fidgety, jerky, whooping thrush." But when Peter Parley, Jacob Abbott, Lydia Maria Child, Mrs. Embury, and Eliza Leslie began to write short stories, the Annuals and periodicals abounded in American scenes and local color.

There was also another great incentive for writers to work for children. This was the demand made for stories from the American Sunday School Union, whose influence upon the character of juvenile literature was a force bearing upon the various writers, and whose growth was coincident with the development of the children's periodical literature.

The American Sunday School Union, an outgrowth of the several religious publication societies, in eighteen hundred and twenty-four began to do more extensive work, and therefore formed a committee to judge and pronounce upon all manuscripts, which American writers were asked to submit.

The sessions of the Sunday-schools were no longer held for illiterate children only. The younger members of each parish or church were found upon its benches each Sunday morning or afternoon. To promote and to impress the religious teaching in these schools, rewards were offered for well-prepared lessons and regular attendance. Also the scholars were encouraged to use the Sunday-school library. For these different purposes many books were needed, but naturally only those stamped with the approval of the clergyman in charge were circulated.

The board of publication appointed by the American Sunday School Union—composed chiefly of clergymen of certain denominations—passed upon the merits of the many manuscripts sent in by piously inclined persons, and edited such of them as proved acceptable. The marginal notes on the pages of the first edition of an old Sunday-school favorite bear witness to the painstaking care of the editors that the leaflets, tracts, and stories poured in from all parts of the country should "shine by reason of the truth contained," and "avoid the least appearance, the most indirect insinuations, of anything which can militate against the strictest ideas of propriety." The tales had also to keep absolutely within the bounds of religion. Many were the stories found lacking in direct religious teaching, or returned because religion was not vitally connected with the plot, to be rewritten or sent elsewhere for publication.

The hundreds of stories turned out in what soon became a mechanical fashion were of two patterns: the one of the good child, a constant attendant upon Sabbath School and Divine Worship, but who died young after converting parent or worldly friend during a painful illness; the other of the unregenerate youth, who turned away from the godly admonition of mother and clergyman, refused to attend Sunday-school, and consequently fell into evil ways leading to the thief's or drunkard's grave. Often a sick mother was introduced to claim emotional attention, or to use as a lay figure upon which to drape Scripture texts as fearful warnings to the black sheep of the family. Indeed, the little reader no sooner began to enjoy the tale of some sweet and gentle girl, or to delight in the mischievous boy, than he was called upon to reflect that early piety portended an early death, and youthful pranks led to a miserable old age. Neither prospect offered much encouragement to hope for a happy life, and from conversations with those brought up on this form of religious culture, it is certain that if a child escaped without becoming morbid and neurotic, there were dark and secret resolves to risk the unpleasant future in favor of a happy present.

The stories, too, presented a somewhat paradoxical familiarity with the ways of a mysterious Providence. This was exceedingly perplexing to the thoughtful child, whose queries as to justice were too often hushed by parent or teacher. In real life, every child expected, even if he did not receive, a tangible reward for doing the right thing; but Providence, according to these authors, immediately caused a good child to become ill unto death. It is not a matter for surprise that the healthy-minded, vigorous child often turned in disgust from the Sunday-school library to search for Cooper's tales of adventure on his father's book-shelves.

The correct and approved child's story, even if not issued under religious auspices, was thoroughly saturated with religion. Whatever may have been the practice of parents in regard to their own reading, they wished that of the nursery to show not only an educational and moral, but a religious tendency. The books for American children therefore divided themselves into three classes: the denominational story, to set forth the doctrines of one church; the educational tale; and the moral narrative of American life.

The denominational stories produced by the several Sunday-school societies were, as has been said, only a kind of scaffolding upon which to build the teachings of the various churches. But their sale was enormous, and a factor to be reckoned with because of their influence upon the educational and moral tales of their period. By eighteen hundred and twenty-seven, fifty-thousand books and tracts had been sent out by one Sunday-school society alone.* There are few things more remarkable in the history of juvenile literature than the growth of the business of the American Sunday School Union. By eighteen hundred and twenty-eight it had issued over seven hundred of these religious trifles, varying from a sixteen-page duodecimo to a small octavo volume; and most of these appear to have been written by Americans trying their inexperienced pens upon a form of literature not then recognized as difficult. The influence of such a flood of tiny books could hardly have been other than morbid, although occasionally there floated down the stream duodecimos which were grasped by little readers with eagerness. Such volumes, one reader of bygone Sunday-school books tells us, glimmered from the dark depths of death and prison scenes, and were passed along with whispered recommendation until their well-

* *Election Day*, p. 71. American Sunday School Union, 1828.

worn covers attracted the eye of the teacher, and were quickly found to be missing from library shelves. Others were commended in their stead, such as described the city boy showing the country cousin the town sights, with most edifying conversation as to their history; or, again, amusement of a light and alluring character was presumably to be found in the story of a little maid who sat upon a footstool at her mother's knee, and while she hemmed the four sides of a handkerchief, listened to the account of missionary enterprises in the dark corners of the earth.

To us of to-day the small illustrations are perhaps the most interesting feature, preserving as they do children's occupations and costumes. In one book we see quaintly frocked and pantaletted girls and much buttoned boys in Sunday-school. In another, entitled "Election Day," are pictured two little lads watching, from the square in front of Independence Hall, the handing in of votes for the President through a window of the famous building—a picture that emphasizes the change in methods of casting the ballot since eighteen hundred and twenty-eight.

That engravers were not always successful when called upon to embellish the pages of the Sunday-school books, many of them easily prove. That the designers of woodcuts were sometimes lacking in imagination when obliged to depict Bible verses can have no better example than the favorite vignette on title-pages portraying "My soul doth magnify the Lord" as a man with a magnifying glass held over a blank space. Perhaps equal in lack of imagination was the often repeated frontispiece of "Mercy streaming from the Cross," illustrated by a large cross with an effulgent rain beating upon the luxuriant tresses of a languishing lady. There were many pictures but little art in the old-fashioned Sunday-school library books.

It was in Philadelphia that one of the first, if not the first children's library was incorporated in 1827 as the Apprentices' Library. Eleven years later this library contained more than two thousand books, and had seven hundred children as patrons. The catalogue of that year is indicative of the prevalence of the Sunday-school book. "Adventures of Lot" precedes the "Affectionate Daughter-in-Law," which is followed by "Anecdotes of Christian Missions" and "An Alarm to Unconverted Sinners." Turning the yellowed pages, we find "Hannah Swanton, the Casco Captive," histories of Bible worthies, the "Infidel Class," "Little Deceiver Reclaimed," "Letters to Little Children," "Juvenile Piety," and "Julianna Oakley." The bookish child of this decade could not escape from the "Reformed Family" and the consumptive little Christian, except by taking refuge in the parents' novels, collections of the British poets and essayists, and the constantly increasing American writings for adults. Perhaps in this way the Sunday-school books may be counted among that long list of such things as are commonly called blessings in disguise.

Aside from the strictly religious tale, the contents of the now considerable output of Harper and Brothers, Mahlon Day, Samuel Wood and Sons of New York; Cottons and Barnard, Lincoln and Edmunds, Lilly, Wait and Company, Munroe and Francis of Boston; Matthew Carey, Conrad and Par-

A Child and her Doll

sons, Morgan and Sons, and Thomas T. Ashe of Philadelphia—to mention but a few of the publishers of juvenile novelties—are convincing proof that booksellers catered to the demand for stories with a strong religious bias. The "New York Weekly," indeed, called attention to Day's books as "maintaining an unbroken tendency to virtue and piety."

When not impossibly pious, these children of anonymous fiction were either insufferable prigs with a steel moral code, or so ill-bred as to be equally impossible and unnatural. The favorite plan of their creators was to follow Miss Edgeworth's device of contrasting the good and naughty infant. The children, too, were often cousins: one, for example, was the son of a gentleman who in his choice of a wife was influenced by strict religious principles; the other boy inherited his disposition from his mother, a lady of bland manners and fine external appearance, but who failed to establish in her offspring "correct principles of virtue, religion, and morality." The author paused at this point in the narrative to discuss the frailties of the lady, before resuming its slender thread. Who to-day could wade through with children the good-goody books of that generation?

Happily, many of the writers for little ones chose to be unknown, for it would be ungenerous to disparage by name these ladies who considered their productions edifying, and in their ingenuousness never dreamed that their stories were devoid of every quality that makes a child's book of value to the child. They were literally unconscious that their tales lacked that simplicity and directness in style, and they themselves that knowledge of human nature, absolutely necessary to construct a pleasing and profitable story. The watchwords of these painstaking ladies were "religion, virtue, and morality," and heedless of everything else, they found oblivion in most cases before they gained recognition from the public they longed to influence.

The decade following eighteen hundred and thirty brought prominently to the foreground six American authors among the many who occasioned brief notice. Of these writers two were men and four were women. Jacob Abbott and Samuel G. Goodrich wrote the educational tales, Abbott largely for the nursery, while Goodrich devoted his attention mainly to books for the little lads at school. The four women, Mrs. Sarah J. Hale, Miss Eliza Leslie, Miss Catharine Sedgwick, and Mrs. Lydia H. Sigourney, wrote mainly for girls, and took American life as their subject. Mrs. Hale wrote much for adults, but when editor of the "Juvenile Miscellany," she made various contributions to it. Yet to-day we know her only by one of her "Poems for Children," published in Boston in eighteen hundred and thirty—"Mary had a Little Lamb."

Mary's lamb has travelled much farther than to school, and has even reached that point when its authorship has been disputed. Quite recently in the "Century Magazine" Mrs. Hale's claim to its composition has been set forth at some length by Mr. Richard W. Hale, who shows clearly her desire when more than ninety years of age to be recognized as the originator of these verses, In fact, "shortly before her death," wrote Mr. Hale, "she directed her son to write emphatically that every poem in her book of eighteen hundred and thirty was of her own composition." Although rarely seen in print, "Mary had a Little Lamb" has outlived all other nursery rhymes of its day; perhaps because it had most truly the quality, unusual at the time, of being told directly and simply—a quality, indeed, that appeals to every generation.

Miss Leslie, like Mrs. Hale, did much editing, beginning on adult gift-books and collections of housewife's receipts, and then giving most of her attention to juvenile literature. As editor Miss Leslie did good work on the "Violet" and the "Pearl," both gift-books for children. She also abridged, edited, and rewrote "The Wonderful Traveller," and the adventures of Munchausen, Gulliver, and Sindbad, heroes often disregarded by this period of lack of imagination and over-supply of educational theories. Also, as a writer of stories for little girls and school-maidens, Eliza Leslie met with warm approval on both sides of the Atlantic.

Undoubtedly the success of Eliza Leslie's "American Girls' Book," modelled after the English "Boy's Own Book," and published in 1831, added to the popularity attained by her earlier work, although of this she was but the compiler.

The "American Girls' Book" was intended for little girls, and by dialogue, the prevailing mode of conveying instruction or amusement, numerous games and plays were described. Already many of the pastimes have gone out of fashion. "Lady Queen Anne" and "Robin 's Alive," "a dangerous game with a lighted stick," are altogether unknown; "Track the Rabbit" has changed its name to "Fox and Geese;" "Hot Buttered Beans" has found a substitute in "Hunt the Thimble;" and "Stir the Mush" has given place to "Going to Jerusalem."

But Miss Leslie did more than preserve for us these old-fashioned games. She has left sketches of children's ways and nature in her various stories for little people. She shared, of course, in the habit of moralizing characteristic of her day, but her children are childish, and her heroines are full of the whims, and have truly the pleasures and natural emotions, of real children.

Miss Leslie began her work for children in eighteen hundred and twenty-seven, when "Atlantic Stories" were published, and as her sketches of child-life appeared one after another, her pen grew more sure in its delineation of characters and her talent was speedily recognized. Even now "Birthday Stories" are worth reading and treasuring because of the pictures of family life eighty years ago. The "Souvenir," for example, is a Christmas tale of old Philadelphia; the "Cadet's Sister" sketches life at West Point, where the author's brother had been a student; while the "Launch of the Frigate" and "Anthony and Clara" tell of customs and amusements quite passed away. The charming description of children shopping for their simple Christmas gifts, the narrative of the boys who paid a poor lad in a bookstore to ornament their "writing-pieces" for more "respectable presents" to parents, the quiet celebration of the day itself, can ill be spared from the history of child life and diversions in America. It is well to be reminded, in these days of complex and expensive amusements, of some of the saner and simpler pleasures enjoyed by children in Miss Leslie's lifetime.

All of this writer's books, moreover, have some real interest, whether it be "Althea Vernon," with the description of summer life and fashions at Far Rockaway (New York's Manhattan Beach of 1830), or "Henrietta Harrison," with its sarcastic reference to the fashionable school where the pupils could sing French songs and Italian operas, but could not be sure of the notes of "Hail Columbia." Or again, the account is worth reading of the heroine's trip to New York from Philadelphia. "Simply habited in a plaid silk frock and Thibet shawl," little Henrietta starts, under her uncle's protection, at five o'clock in the morning to take the boat for Bordentown, New Jersey. There she has her first experience of a railway train, and looks out of the window "at all the velocity of the train will allow her to see." At Heightstown small children meet the train with fruit and cakes to sell to hungry travellers. And finally comes the wonderful voyage from Amboy to the Battery in New York, which is not reached until night has fallen.

This is the simple explanation as to why Eliza Leslie's books met with so generous a reception: they were full of the incidents which children love, and unusually free from the affectations of the pious fictitious heroine.

The stories of Miss Catharine Sedgwick also received most favorable criticism, and in point of style were certainly better than Miss Leslie's. Her reputation as a literary woman was more than national, and "Redwood," one of her best novels, was attributed in France to Fenimore Cooper, when it appeared anonymously in eighteen hundred and twenty-four. Miss Sedgwick's novels, however, pass out of nursery comprehension in the first chapters, although these were full of a healthy New England atmosphere, with coasting parties and picnics, Indians and gypsies, nowhere else better described.

The same tone pervades her contributions to the "Juvenile Miscellany," the "Token," and the "Youth's Keepsake," together with her best-known children's books, "Stories for Children," "A Well Spent Hour," and "A Love Token for Children."

In contrast to Mrs. Sherwood's still popular "Fairchild Family," Catharine Sedgwick's stories breathe a sunny, invigorating atmosphere, abounding in local incidents, and vigorous in delineation of types then plentiful in New England. "She has fallen," wrote one admirer, most truthfully, in the "North American Review" of 1827,—"she has fallen upon the view, from which the treasures of our future literature are to be wrought. A literature to have real freshness must be moulded by the influences of the society where it had its origin. Letters thrive, when they are at home in the soil. Miss Sedgwick's imaginations have such vigor and bloom because they are not exotics." Another reviewer, aroused by English criticism of the social life in America, and full of the much vaunted theory that "all men are equal," rejoiced in the author's attitude towards the so-called "help" in New England families in contrast to Miss More's portrayal of the English child's condescension towards inferiors, which he thought unsuitable to set before the children in America.

All Miss Sedgwick's stories were the product of her own keen intelligence and observation, and not written in imitation of Miss More, Miss Edgeworth, or Mrs. Sherwood, as were the anonymous tales of "Little Lucy; or, the Pleasant Day," or "Little Helen; a Day in the Life of a Naughty Girl." They preached, indeed, at length, but the preaching could be skipped by interested readers, and unlike the work of many contemporaries, there was always a thread to take up.

Mrs. Lydia H. Sigourney, another favorite contributor to magazines, collected her "Poetry for Children" into a volume bearing this title, in eighteen hundred and thirty-four, and published "Tales and Essays" in the same year. These were followed two years later by "Olive Buds," and thereafter at intervals she brought out several other books, none of which have now any interest except as examples of juvenile literature that had once a decided vogue and could safely be bought for the Sunday-school library.

The names of Mrs. Anna M. Wells, Mrs. Frances S. Osgood, Mrs. Farrar, Mrs. Eliza L. Follen, and Mrs. Seba Smith were all well beloved by children eighty years ago, and their writings, if long since lost sight of, at least added their quota to the children's publications which were distinctly American.

If the quantity of books sold is any indication of the popularity of an author's work, nothing produced by any of these ladies is to be compared with the "Tales of Peter Parley" and the "Rollo Books" of Jacob Abbott.

The tendency to instruct while endeavoring to entertain was remodelled by these men, who in after years had a host of imitators. Great visions of good to children had overtaken dreams of making children good, with the result that William Darton's conversational method of instruction was compounded with Miss Edgeworth's educational theories and elaborated after the manner of Hannah More. Samuel Goodrich, at least, confessed that his many tales were the direct result of a conversation with Miss More, whom, because of his admiration for her books, he made an effort to meet when in England in eighteen hundred and twenty-three. While talking with the old lady about her "Shepherd of Salisbury Plain," the idea came to Mr. Goodrich that he, himself, might write for American children and make good use of her method of introducing much detail in description. As a child he had not found the few toy-books within his reach either amusing or interesting, with the exception of this Englishwoman's writings. He resolved that the growing generation should be better served, but little dreamed of the unprecedented success, as far as popularity was concerned, that the result of his determination would prove.

After his return to America, the immediate favorable reception of the "Token," under Goodrich's direction, led to the publication in the same year (1828) of "Peter Parley's Tales about America," followed by "Tales about Europe." At this date of retrospection the first volume seems in many ways the best of any of the numerous books by the same author. The boy hero, taken as a child companion upon a journey through several states, met with adventures among Indians upon the frontiers, and saw places of historical significance. Every incident is told in imitation of Miss More, with that detailed description which Goodrich had found so fascinating. If a little overdone in this respect, the narrative has certainly a freshness sadly deficient in many later volumes. Even the second tale seems to lack the engaging spontaneity of the first, and already to grow didactic and recitative rather than personal. But both met with an equally generous and appreciative reception. Parley's educational tales were undoubtedly the American pioneers in what may be readily styled the "travelogue" manner used in later years by Elbridge Brooks and many other writers for little people. These early attempts of Parley's to educate the young reader were followed by one hundred others, which sold like hot cakes. Of some tales the sales reached a total of fifty thousand in one year, while it is estimated that seven million of Peter Parley's "Histories" and "Tales" were sold before the admiration of their style and qualities waned.

Peter Parley took his heroes far afield. Jacob Abbott adopted another plan of instruction in the majority of his books. Beginning in eighteen hundred and thirty-four with the "Young Christian Series," the Reverend Mr. Abbott soon had readers in England, Scotland, Germany, France, Holland, and India, where many of his volumes were translated and republished. In the "Rollo Books" and "Franconia" an attempt was made to answer many of the questions that children of each century pour out to astonish and confound their elders. The child reader saw nothing incongruous in the remarkable wisdom and maturity of Mary Bell and Beechnut, who could give advice and information with equal glibness. The advice, moreover, was often worth following, and the knowledge occasionally worth having; and the little one swallowed chunks of morals and morsels of learning without realizing that he was doing so. Most of both was speedily forgotten, but many adults in after years were unconsciously indebted to Goodrich and Abbott for some familiarity with foreign countries, some interest in natural science.

Notwithstanding the immense demand for American stories, there was fortunately still some doubt as to whether this remodelled form of instructive amusement and moral story-book literature did not lack certain wholesome features characteristic of the days when fairies and folklore, and Newbery's gilt volumes, had plenty of room on the nursery table. "I cannot very well tell," wrote the editor of the "Fairy Book"* in 1836,—"I cannot very well tell why it is that the good old histories and tales, which used to be given to young people for their amusement and instruction, as soon as they could read, have of late years gone quite out of fashion in this country. In former days there was a worthy English bookseller, one Mr. Newbery, who used to print thousands of nice little volumes of such stories, which, as he solemnly declared in print in the books themselves, he gave away to all little boys and girls, charging them only a sixpenny for the gold covers. These of course no one could be so unreasonable as to wish him to furnish at his own expense. . . . Yet in the last generation, American boys and girls (the fathers and mothers, grandfathers and grandmothers of the present generation) were not wholly dependent upon Mr. Newbery of St. Paul's church-yard, though they knew him well and loved him much. The great Benjamin Franklin, when a printer in Philadelphia, did not disdain to print divers of Newbery's books adorned with cuts in the likeness of his, though it must be confessed somewhat inferior.† Yet rude as they were, they were probably the first things in the way of pictures that West and

* Mr. G. C. Verplanck was probably the editor of this book, published by Harper & Bros.

† This statement the writer has been unable to verify.

Copley ever beheld, and so instilled into those future painters, the rudiments of that art by which they afterwards became so eminent themselves, and conferred such honour upon their native country. In somewhat later time there were the worthy Hugh Gaine, at the Sign of the Bible and Crown in Pearl street, and the patriotic Samuel Loudon, and the genuine and unadulterated New Yorker, Evert Duyckinck, besides others in Boston and Philadelphia, who trod in the steps of Newbery, and supplied the infant mind with its first and sweetest literary food. The munificent Newbery, and the pious and loyal Hugh Gaine, and the patriotic Samuel Loudon are departed. Banks now abound and brokers swarm where Loudon erst printed, and many millions worth of silk and woolen goods are every year sold where Gaine vended his big Bibles and his little story-books. They are all gone; the glittering covers and their more brilliant contents, the tales of wonder and enchantment, the father's best reward for merit, the good grandmother's most prized presents. They are gone—the cheap delight of childhood, the unbought grace of boyhood, the dearest, freshest, and most unfading recollections of maturer life. They are gone—and in their stead has succeeded a swarm of geological catechisms, entomological primers, and tales of political economy—dismal trash, all of them; something half-way between stupid story-books and bad school-books; being so ingeniously written as to be unfit for any useful purpose in school and too dull for any entertainment out of it."

This is practically Charles Lamb's lament of some thirty years before. Lamb had despised the learned Charles, Mrs.

Barbauld's peg upon which to hang instruction, and now an American Shakespeare lover found the use of toy-books as mechanical guides to knowledge for nursery inmates equally deplorable.

Yet an age so in love with the acquirement of solid facts as to produce a Parley and an Abbott was the period when the most famous of all nursery books was brought out from the dark corner into which it had been swept by the theories of two generations, and presented once again as "The Only True Mother Goose Melodies."

The origin of Mother Goose as the protecting genius of the various familiar jingles has been an interesting field of speculation and research. The claim for Boston as the birthplace of their sponsor has long ago been proved a poor one, and now seems likely to have been an ingenious form of advertisement. But Boston undoubtedly did once again make popular, at least in America, the lullabies and rhymes repeated for centuries around French or English firesides.

The history of Mother Goose and her brood is a long one. "Mother Goose," writes Mr. Walter T. Field, "began her existence as the raconteuse of fairy tales, not as the nursery poetess. As La Mère Oye she told stories to French children more than two hundred and fifty years ago." According to the researches made by Mr. Field in the literature of Mother Goose, "the earliest date at which Mother Goose appears as the author of children's stories is 1667, when Charles Perrault, a distinguished French littérateur, published in Paris a little book of tales which he had during that and the preceding year contributed to a magazine known as 'Moejen's Recueil,' printed at The Hague. This book is entitled 'Histoires ou Contes du Tems Passé, avec des Moralitez,' and has a frontispiece in which an old woman is pictured, telling stories to a family group by the fireside while in the background are the words in large characters, 'Contes de ma Mère l'Oye.'"

It seems, however, to have been John Newbery's publishing-house that made Mother Goose sponsor for the ditties in much the form in which we now have them. In Newbery's collection of "Melodies" there were numerous footnotes burlesquing Dr. Johnson and his dictionary, together with jests upon the moralizing habit prevalent among authors. There is evidence that Goldsmith wrote many of these notes when doing hack-work for the famous publisher in St. Paul's Churchyard. It is known, for instance, that in January, 1760, Goldsmith celebrated the production of his "Good Natur'd Man" by dining his friends at an inn. During the feast he sang his favorite song, said to be

> "There was an old woman tos't up in a blanket,
> Seventy times as high as the moon."

This was introduced quite irrelevantly in the preface to "Mother Goose's Melodies," but with the apology that it was a favorite with the editor. There is also the often quoted remark of Miss Hawkins as confirming Goldsmith's editorship: "I little thought what I should have to boast, when Goldsmith taught me to play Jack and Jill, by two bits of paper on his fingers." But neither of these statements seems to have more weight in solving the mystery of the editor's name than the evidence of the whimsically satirical notes themselves. How like the author of the "Vicar of Wakefield" and the children's "Fables in Verse" is this remark underneath:

"'There was an old Woman who liv'd under a hill,
And if she 's not gone, she lives there still.'

"This is a self evident Proposition, which is the very essence of Truth. She lived under the hill, and if she 's not gone, she lives there still. Nobody will presume to contradict this. *Croesa.*"

And is not this also a good-natured imitation of that kind of seriously intended information which Mr. Edgeworth inserted some thirty years later in "Harry and Lucy:" "Dry, what is not wet"? Again this note is appended to

"See Saw Margery Daw
Jacky shall have a new master:"

"It is a mean and scandalous Practise in Authors to put Notes to Things that deserve no Notice." Who except Goldsmith was capable of this vein of humor?

When Munroe and Francis in Boston undertook about eighteen hundred and twenty-four to republish these old-fashioned rhymes, in the practice of the current theory that everything must be simplified, they omitted all these notes and changed many of the "Melodies." Sir Walter Scott's "Donnel Dhu" was included, and the beautiful Shakespeare selections, "When Daffodils begin to 'pear," "When the Bee sucks," etc., were omitted. Doubtless the American editors thought that they had vastly improved upon the Newbery publication in every word changed and every line omitted. In reality, they deprived the nursery of much that might well have remained as it was, although certain expressions were very properly altered. In a negative manner they did one surprising and fortunate thing: in leaving out the amusing notes they did not attempt to replace them, and consequently the nursery had one book free from that advice and precept, which in other verse for children resulted in persistent nagging. The illustrations were entirely redrawn, and Abel Bowen and Nathaniel Dearborn were asked to do the engraving for this Americanized edition.

Of the poetry written in America for children before eighteen hundred and forty there is little that need be said. Much of it was entirely religious in character and most of it was colorless and dreary stuff. The "Child's Gem" of eighteen hundred and thirty-eight, considered a treasury of precious verse by one reviewer, and issued in embossed morocco binding, was characteristic of many contemporary *poems*, in which nature was forced to exude precepts of virtue and industry. The following stanzas are no exception to the general tone of the contents of practically every book entitled "Poetry for Children:"

> "'Be good, little Edmund,' your mother will say,
> She will whisper it soft in your ear,
> And often repeat it, by night and by day
> That you may not forget it, my dear.
>
> "And the ant at its work, and the flower-loving bee
> And the sweet little bird in the wood
> As it warbles its song, from its nest in the tree,
> Seems to say, 'little Eddy be good.'"

The change in the character of the children's books written by Americans had begun to be seriously noticed in England. Although there were still many importations (such as the series written by Mrs. Sherwood), there was some inclination to resent the stocking of American booksellers' shelves by the work of local talent, much to the detriment of English publishers' pockets. The literary critics took up the subject, and thought themselves justified in disparaging many of the American books which found also ready sale on English book-counters. The religious books underwent scathing criticism, possibly not undeserved, except that the English productions of the same order and time make it now appear that it was but the pot calling the kettle black. Almost as much fault was found with the story-books. It apparently mattered little that the tables were now turned and British publishers were pirating American tales as freely and successfully as Thomas and Philadelphia printers had in former years made use of Newbery's, and Darton and Harvey's, juvenile novelties in book ware.

In the "Quarterly Review" of 1843, in an article entitled "Books for Children," the writer found much cause for complaint in regard to stories then all too conspicuous in bookshops in England. "The same egregious mistakes," said the critic, "as to the nature of a child's understanding—the same explanations, which are all but indelicate, and always profane—seem to pervade all these American mentors; and of a number by Peter Parley, Abbott, Todd, &c., it matters little which we take up." "Under the name of Peter Parley," continued the disgruntled gentleman, after finding only malicious evil in poor Mr. Todd's efforts to explain religious doctrines, "such a number of juvenile schoolbooks are current—some greatly altered from the originals and many more by *adopters* of *Mr. Goodrich's* pseudonym

—that it becomes difficult to measure the merits or demerits of the said *magnus parens*, Goodrich." Liberal quotations followed from "Peter Parley's Farewell," which was censured as palling to the mind of those familiar with the English sources from which the facts had been irreverently culled.

The reviewer then passed on to another section of "American abominations" which "seem to have some claim to popularity since they are easily sold." "These," continued the anonymous critic, "are works not of amusement—those we shall touch upon later—but of that half-and-half description where instruction blows with a side wind. . . . Accordingly after impatient investigation of an immense number of little tomes, we are come to the conclusion that they may be briefly classified—firstly, as containing such information as any child in average life who can speak plainly is likely to be possessed of; and secondly, such as when acquired is not worth having."

To this second class of book the Reverend Mr. Abbott's "Rollo Books" were unhesitatingly consigned. They were regarded as curiosities for "mere occupation of the eye, and utter stagnation of the thoughts, full of empty minutiae with all the rules of common sense set aside."

Next the writer considered the style of those Americans who persuaded shillings from English pockets by "ingeniously contrived series which rendered the purchase of a single volume by no means so recommendable as that of all." The "uncouth phraseology, crack-jack words, and puritan derived words are nationalized and therefore do not permit cavilling," continued the reviewer, dismayed and disgusted that it was necessary to warn his public, "but their children never did, or perhaps never will, hear any other language; and it is to be hoped they *understand* it. At all events, we have nothing to do but keep ours from it, believing firmly that early familiarity with refined and beautiful forms . . . is one of the greatest safeguards against evil, if not necessary to good."

However, the critic did not close his article without a good word for those ladies in whose books we ourselves have found merit. "Their works of amusement" he considered admirable, "when not laden with more religion than the tale can hold in solution. Miss Sedgwick takes a high place for powers of description and traits of nature, though her language is so studded with Americanisms as much to mar the pleasure and perplex the mind of an English reader. Besides this lady, Mrs. Sigourney and Mrs. Seba Smith may be mentioned. The former, especially, to all other gifts adds a refinement, and nationality of subject, with a knowledge of life, which some of her poetical pieces led us to expect. Indeed the little Americans have little occasion to go begging to the history or tradition ot other nations for topics of interest."

The "Westminster Review" of eighteen hundred and forty was also in doubt "whether all this Americanism [such as Parley's 'Tales' contained] is desirable for English children, were it," writes the critic, "only for them we keep the 'pure well of English undefiled,' and cannot at all admire the improvements which it pleases that go-ahead nation to claim the right of making in our common tongue: unwisely enough as regards themselves, we think, for one of the elements in the power of a nation is the wide spread of its language."

This same criticism was made again and again about the style of American writers for adults, so that it is little wonder the children's books received no unqualified praise. But Americanisms were not the worst feature of the "inundation of American children's books," which because of their novelty threatened to swamp the "higher class" English. They were feared because of the "multitude of false notions likely to be derived from them, the more so as the similarity of name and language prevents children from being on their guard, and from remembering that the representations that they read are by foreigners." It was the American view of English institutions (presented in story-book form) which rankled in the British breast as a "condescending tenderness of the free nation towards the monarchical régime" from which at any cost the English child must be guarded. In this respect Peter Parley was the worst offender, and was regarded as "a sad purveyor of slip-slop, and no matter how amusing, ignorant of his subject." That gentleman, meanwhile, read the criticisms and went on making "bread and butter," while he scowled at the English across the water, who criticised, but pirated as fast as he published in America.

Gentle Miss Eliza Leslie received altogether different treatment in this review of American juvenile literature. She was considered "good everywhere, and particularly so for the meridian in which her tales were placed;" and we quite agree with the reviewer who considered it well worth while to quote long paragraphs from her "Tell Tale" to show its character and "truly useful lesson." "To America," continued this writer, "we also owe a host of little books, that bring together the literature of childhood and the people; as 'Home,' 'Live and Let Live' [by Miss Sedgwick], &c., but excellent in intention as they are, we have our doubts, as to the general reception they will meet in this country while so much of more exciting and elegant food is at hand." Even if the food of amusement in England appeared to the British mind more spiced and more *elegant*, neither Miss Leslie's nor Miss Sedgwick's fictitious children were ever anaemic puppets without wills of their own,—a type made familiar by Miss Edgeworth and persisted in by her admirers and successors,—but vitalized little creatures, who acted to some degree, at least, like the average child who loved their histories and named her dolls after favorite characters.

To-day these English criticisms are only of value as showing that the American story-book was no longer imitating the English tale, but was developing, by reason of the impress of differing social forces, a new type. Its faults do not prevent us from seeing that the spirit expressed in this juvenile literature is that of a new nation feeling its own way, and making known its purpose in its own manner. While we smile at sedulous endeavors of the serious-minded writers to present their convictions, educational, religious, or moral, in palatable form, and to consider children always as a race apart, whose natural actions were invariably sinful, we still read between the lines that these writers were really interested in the welfare of the American child; and that they were working according to the accepted theories of the third decade of the nineteenth

The Little Runaway

century as to the constituents of a juvenile library which, while "judicious and attractive, should also blend instruction with innocent amusement."

And now as we have reached the point in the history of the American story-book when it is popular at least in both English-speaking countries, if not altogether satisfactory to either, what can be said of the value of this juvenile literature of amusement which has developed on the tiny pages of well-worn volumes? If, of all the books written for children by Americans seventy-five years and more ago, only Nathaniel Hawthorne's "Wonder Book" has survived to the present generation; of all the verse produced, only the simple rhyme, "Mary had a Little Lamb," and Clement Moore's "The Night before Christmas" are still quoted, has their history any value to-day?

If we consider that there is nothing more rare in the fiction of any nation than the popular child's story that endures; nothing more unusual than the successful well-written juvenile tale, we can perhaps find a value not to be reckoned by the survival or literary character of these old-fashioned books, but in their silent testimony to the influence of the progress of social forces at work even upon so small a thing as a child's toy-book. The successful well-written child's book has been rare, because it has been too often the object rather than the manner of writing that has been considered of importance; because it has been the aim of all writers either to "improve in goodness" the young reader, as when, two hundred years ago, Cotton Mather penned "Good Lessons" for his infant son to learn at school, or, to quote the editor of "Affection's Gift" (published a century and a quarter later), it has been for the purpose of "imparting moral precepts and elevated sentiments, of uniting instruction and amusement, through the fascinating mediums of interesting narrative and harmony of numbers."

The result of both intentions has been a collection of dingy or faded duodecimos containing a series of impressions of what each generation thought good, religiously, morally, and educationally, for little folk. If few of them shed any light upon child nature in those long-ago days, many throw shafts of illumination upon the change and progress in American ideals and thought concerning the welfare of children. As has already been said, the press supplied what the public taste demanded, and if the writers produced for earlier generations of children what may now be considered lumber, the press of more modern date has not progressed so far in this field of literature as to make it in any degree certain that our children's treasures may not be consigned to an equal oblivion. For these too are but composites made by superimposing the latest fads or theories as to instructive amusement of children upon those of previous generations of toy-books. Most of what was once considered the "perfume of youth and freshness" in a literary way has been discarded as dry and unprofitable, mistaken or deceptive; and yet, after all has been said by way of criticism of methods and subjects, these chap-books, magazines, gift and story books form our best if blurred pictures of the amusements and daily life of the old-time American child.

We are learning also to prize these small "Histories" as part of the progress of the arts of book-making and illustration, and of the growth of the business of publishing in America; and already we are aware of the fulfilment of what was called by one old bookseller, "Tom Thumb's Maxim in Trade and Politics:" "He who buys this book for Two-pence, and lays it up till it is worth Three-pence, may get an hundred per cent by the bargain."

Index

INDEX

Index

Index

Index

Index